Advanced Praise for

An Irreligious Life:

How to Starve Religion and Feed Life

"Glenn Hager's spiritual journey takes readers through a desolate landscape of religious arrogance, divisiveness, and self-righteousness. It will be an all-too-familiar journey for many who have been alienated or abandoned by American Christianity. However, Hager's destination is one of hope and healing. He knows that where Christianity has failed is the place where Jesus meets us and lifts us up."

- **Doug Worgul**, author of *Thin Blue Smoke* (Burnside Books)

"Glenn Hager is a former pastor who loves the Church. Like so many leaders we hear from at Key Life Network, that love went unrequited. Glenn's passion for the truth Jesus proclaimed and incarnated eventually made him an outsider among those he worked so hard to serve. Really, how else could it go for anyone who follows the carpenter from Nazareth? Jesus revealed that even God is an outsider among his own people. While he got close, Glenn should be grateful he wasn't crucified. If you've been burned by the institutional church, read this book to find you are not alone and, in fact, much closer to God than you may think."

- **Erik Guzman**, Erik Guzman, Producer and Vice President of Communications for the Key Life Network

"If you have found yourself on the fringes of faith, if you've left church, if you are tired of the religious rules, "shoulds", and hypocrisy of organized religion, if you long to follow Jesus but aren't sure how to anymore, you'll find hope in Glenn Hager's Irreligious Faith. His story of moving from dutiful Christian insider to an on the fringe outsider will deeply encourage those who are tired of the system but long for a renewed and active faith. In his words, you'll find ideas and a challenge for "the gusty lovers of Jesus to break from the herd and wander into the rich pasture lands of freedom."

- **Kathy Escobar**, Co-Pastor of The Refuge and author of *Down We Go: Living into the Wild Ways of Jesus* (Civitas Press)

"*An Irreligious Faith* is a warm and honest reflection of Glenn Hager's journey from a young pastor committed to Jesus and the evangelical church to an older, wiser, compassionate, unemployed pastor who still hungers to follow Jesus. Hager invites us into his own passionate story of following Jesus as he discerns the difference between the religious baggage in the evangelical community and the core message and practice of Jesus. He reflects on his own religious wounds and turns to reconsidering Jesus-centered wisdom as the way forward. As someone who is close to Hager's age, I'm impressed with his enduring passion to follow Jesus through and beyond religious cynicism. We need more reflective stories which reveal hard-earned wisdom like *An Irreligious Faith*. This book will provoke you to a passionate faith, toward what really matters. I highly recommend it."

- **Dan J. Brennan**, author of *Sacred Unions, Sacred Passions: Engaging the Mystery of Friendship Between Men and Women* (Faith Dance Publishing)

"*An Irreligious Faith* is a portrait of a pastor and his journey from church leader to churchless wanderer. Breaking out of the cage of religion, Glenn stumbled onto new discoveries of how to follow Jesus and serve communities apart from churchified codes and rigid traditions. This is his manifesto of how he starved religion and in doing so, found the life of faith he longed for all of his life. Church exiles, especially exiled pastors and ministry leaders, will relate to Glenn's story and in doing so find camaraderie in the growing tribe of the irreligious Jesus followers."

- **Pam Hogeweide**, blogger and author of *Unladylike: Resisting the Injustice of Inequality in the Church* (Civitas Press)

"Using his own personal story as a foundation, Glenn Hager writes insightfully about this thing we call "church." He shows that while some people may have left the church as an organization, they have not left the church as an organism. Though they may no longer sit in a pew, they are still in a living, breathing, growing relationship with Jesus and with others. In *An Irreligious Faith*, Glenn Hager calls us to live our faith in a way that looks a lot like Jesus."

- **Jeremy Myers**, Author and Blogger at TillHeComes.org

"Try to imagine this scene. It's 12 Billion BC. The Father, Son and Spirit are having a beer, planning how Jesus will save the world when The Holy Spirit has an unusual revelation. "Hey you guys I just realized that by 2014 Jesus will be the leader of the world's largest religion, how cool is that." All joking aside, the way Christians presume that the religion called Christianity was Jesus' idea is just as ludicrous. Jesus has no more to do with Christianity than he does with Buddhism or Islam. He does not look at the outward appearance but at the heart. His new social realism is what he calls the Kingdom. Afred Loisy once observed that "Jesus called for the Kingdom and the Church appeared." If new voices like Glenn Hager's rise to the surface we may see the coming of the Kingdom sooner than we thought."

- **Jim Henderson**, Executive Producer Jim Henderson Presents and author of *Jim and Casper Go to Church* and *Saving Casper*

"In his book, *An Irreligious Faith*, Glenn Hager describes the process that moved him beyond the boundaries of the church as an institution and into uncharted territory. He gives voice to the frustrations of many Christians who want to focus on love and the example of Jesus rather than on what one has to believe. Following Jesus means turning love into action. There's no simple or single answer to reforming the church. We'll begin by encouraging groups of people to attempt new ways of serving that they determine is best in their setting and not worrying if they conform to a prescribed plan determined by a distant hierarchy. As we build on our successes and learn from our failures, we will become more effective in being the body of Christ in the world."

- **Paul W. Meier**, author of the *In Living Color* series – *The Lord's Prayer* and *The Beatitudes* (Malcolm Creek Publishing)

"I identify strongly with Glenn Hager, having been a pastor who left the ministry and the church. With a mixture of his own experiences, research, and conclusions, Glenn weaves a compelling and convincing story that many who struggle with the church will resonate with."

- **David Hayward**, the "nakedpastor" blog and theLastingSupper.com community

An Irreligious Faith

How to Starve Religion and Feed Life

Glenn Hager

COMMUNITAS BOOKS
An Irreligious Faith: How to Starve Religion and Feed Life
Glenn Hager

General Editor: Erin Word
Cover Design: Robert Crum

ISBN: 0615960553
ISBN 13: 9780615960555
Library of Congress Control Number: 2014903432
CreateSpace Independent Publishing Platform
North Charleston, South Carolina

Published in the United States by Communitas Books.

Version 1.1
Printed by CreateSpace, a DBA of the On-Demand Publishing, LLC

Acknowledgements

Each of these people had a part in encouraging me, stirring me, equipping me, and assisting me, until I finally wrote and published these words.

Erin Word was the first person to get excited about this project and that gave me the courage to finish it. Her editing made it a better book. Thankfully, one of us knows what a split infinitive is. There is a good possibility we will team up again in the future.

Bob Crum uncovered the picture in my head and put it on the cover of this book. I appreciate his bearing with me through the long development process.

Stephanie Chandler and The Nonfiction Authors Association were the source for almost everything I learned about independent publishing and book marketing. The speakers at the Nonfiction Writers Conference and their resources were invaluable to me.

Erik Guzman took a chance on a guy who approached him out of the blue to do The Collective Podcast. He added a professional-sounding, insightful voice to the show; along with his very own brand of Merry Monk-ness. I loved our chats "off the air," too.

Steve Brown kept me going during the difficult times. When I listened to him on *Steve Brown, Etc.,* I was enlightened, encouraged, and usually, amused. When I met him, I discovered he is not only an unapologetic champion of grace, but also, a very gracious person.

The writers of Communitas Collective, about twenty of them, wrote about their journey into unknown territory as a way to assist other travelers who would walk down a similar road. I learned from each of them.

To Patty

You have always been my patient, faithful, forgiving
companion on this journey of a countless unexpected
twists and turns. Thank God, I never travel alone.
I love you!

Contents

Introduction

The visionary is the one who brings his or her voice into the world and who refuses to edit, rehearse, perform, or hide. It is the visionary who knows that the power of creativity is aligned with authenticity.
- Angeles Arrien

Condensed common sense; that's what lies ahead as you read this book. (Or, at least, that's my opinion.) It's not full of meticulous research. Rather, it is based upon experience and observation, including a lifetime of church involvement and over two decades of pastoral service. In stark contrast to all those years of church work, I have spent the last twelve years trying to figure out how to follow Jesus in spite of a growing frustration with the church I have loved for so long.

Because the book has a condensed feel and doesn't beat around the bush, those of you who share my frustration will probably enjoy its directness. But, for people who are comfortable with more conventional ways of doing church, this book might be a little much. I ask you to stir in a lot of grace and a willingness to give me the benefit of the doubt as you read.

I have a long-term daily habit of listening to NPR and watching Fox News. It's disturbing to admit my NPR habit, because half of the people in America will think I am an idiot.

It's disturbing to admit my Fox News habit, because the other half of the population will think I am an idiot. Now that I have owned up to both, everyone thinks I am an idiot!

The point is, it's important to get our news from more than one source, and it's important to listen to the "other side." I try to write in a way that represents a substantial movement of people who love Jesus and love the church, but have issues with what the church has become. So, if you have a strong commitment to the institutional church, you will probably consider what I have to say as coming from the "other side." I hope you will find it in your heart to try to understand what those who feel disenfranchised by the church are saying, because they are your brothers and sisters.

Why did I write this book?

Honestly, only a short time before I wrote this book, I had decided to put my writing about the church behind me. I had been writing about it on a blog for over six years, and I was tired of it. Much of my experience was so painful, especially the last few years, that I didn't want to re-visit it yet another time. However, I had a strong feeling my story needed to be told for the sake of all of those who are on a similar path.

Who is it for?

Throughout my journey, I have found companions and become acquainted with their stories. These people helped me through the rough spots. Now, it is my turn to help my fellow travelers, to give them a heads-up about some of the things they may find on their journey.

This book is for the "questioners"; those who may remain in the church but have certain frustrations they are trying to sort out. I was one of you, and I have felt your inner conflict for several years.

It's for the "leavers"; those who have left the institutional church and are trying to make sense of their life, their faith, and their relationships in the aftermath of their bold decision. This is where I have found myself the last few years.

The book is for former pastors, who, for one reason or another, are no longer with the church. I am one of you, and I have struggled long and hard to find something which captures my soul like my previous work.

The book is for current pastors, church leaders, and everyone else who loves the church and wants it to be better. I can't shake my love of the church, but I know it can be better.

Lastly, it's for those who have never darkened the church's doorway because it seems like Jesus and the church are miles apart. My heart goes out to you. I hope this helps to make some sense of your own spiritual longings.

You will find that I write in one section about how church could make some shifts to get back on track with its mission, and in another section I write about how to forge a faith without involvement in an institutional church. If that seems a little contrary, it is because I believe in the validity of both paths. We are all at different places in our journey.

This book is for anyone who loves the church but has some issues with it. It's for people who want to bring the revolutionary ways of Jesus into their present daily experience. It's for those who are looking for a stripped-down, raw and real way to join in Jesus' kingdom right now. It's for people who are tired of carrying around the baggage of Christendom and are longing for a faith expression that makes sense. It's for people who want to jettison judgmentalism and replace it with love for those who live on the fringes of acceptability. It's for people who are no longer willing to outsource their spiritual expression to an organization, realizing they are responsible for their own spirituality and growth. It's for people who want to reunite faith and life, instead of trying to compartmentalize them. It's for people who know Jesus is the model for living a life of radical love.

What's in it?

I'll begin by telling you my story because it will provide an important backdrop for all that follows. You'll see how my relationship with the church gave my life meaning, how I was the ultimate church insider, how I tried to bring change from within, and how I eventually became an outsider. It's a pretty weird story, but I suspect parts of it will resonate with you.

I'll move on to talk about the surprising ways of Jesus, who preferred the outcasts of society over the religious. He was a strange Messiah, a chronic rule breaker who associated with everyone who was considered untouchable by his culture. He was a counter-intuitive Savior who constantly insulted the powerful religious leaders who eventually had him put to death.

Since I believe there is hope for the institutional church, I will take a look at some shifts the church could make to look a little more like Jesus. I also consider the practical solution side of each of the suggestions.

The last part of the book is dedicated to those who have left church as you have known it. You are not malcontents or heretics; you're pioneers who have assumed responsibility for your own spiritual expression. I believe you will lead the church and the kingdom into the future.

You can skip around between sections, because each one stands on its own.

At the end of the last three sections there is a portion I've called "Engage," which is designed to help you kick-start living out the principles from those sections of the book.

Why *An Irreligious Faith?*

What's with the title? On your Facebook profile, there is this place where you are asked to indicate your religious views. I tried to think of something to accurately describe mine, but terms like, "Catholic," "Protestant," and "Evangelical" just didn't fit. So, I tried to think of something short, but true, to describe me. I came up with "Irreligious Lover of Jesus." "Irreligious," because religion is not a part of my faith. "Jesus," because he is my faith and he informs my life. "Lover," because sometimes I am not a very good follower, but I really do love him.

I am writing about a faith that is experienced and lived. Religion pulls us out of regular life for our faith expression. I am writing about merging faith and life into something real and integrated. Religion decides who is in and who is out. I am trying to figure out how to love everybody. (Admittedly, it's a significant challenge for me.) Religion is a label, a brand. I am writing about a way of living. Religion becomes a power center in the culture, and even becomes a breeding ground for extremists and terrorists. I am trying to unlock the power of loving like Jesus. Religion is based upon knowledge and ritual and can lead to pride, arrogance, and hatred. I am trying to find something more meaningful, more real, and more Jesus-like.

I certainly don't have everything figured out, and I don't believe there is only one way of following Jesus that works for everybody, but I know we can do better. There has to be a way to live in the way of Jesus as a natural part of our daily life, helping us to love those around us. I call it an irreligious faith.

Part 1

An Irreligious Journey:
Coerced into Freedom

"The world for which you have been so artfully pre-
pared is being taken from you, by the grace of God."
- Walter Bruggemann

I loved Jesus, I loved the church, and I really loved being a pastor, but I almost lost my own soul in the process. Being a pastor
was my professional identity and, sadly, my personal identity, as
well. When it was ripped away, I was utterly lost and couldn't
find my way forward for several years. Maybe, it wasn't Jesus I
loved so much as it was the church and being the go-to guy.

Eventually, things flip-flopped in my life, and I found
myself on the other side of the table, arguing with pastors and
Christian leaders until I was branded a troublemaker. I prefer
the term "outsider."

one

Impatient Novice

There I was, eighteen years old with bushy hair and super long sideburns, I had a large Bible in my left hand, and my raised right hand was clenched into a preacher's fist. I was wearing my bright red corduroy jacket and my red and black suede shoes. It sounds hideous now, but I was a fashionable young preacher in the seventies. Finally, I knew who I was and what I must do. My calling to be a pastor fit me so well it became like a malignant growth, enveloping my total identity. But, I loved it! I'll get back to that in a little bit.

The Nerd

As a child, I was coddled by my sweet but overprotective mother. My dad was often away, working extra shifts as a bus driver to support his family. I felt suffocated as a child, and I have no memories of friends spending the night or me staying with them. So, I was a bit of a loner and a misfit.

In my ghetto-ish elementary school, I began my social life with certain advantages. I was a smart, good looking kid, who was financially better off than most of my school mates. But, my greatest advantage was that I looked tough. I wasn't tough, but I looked the part.

Those traits carried me through the early years, but eventually the overprotectiveness caught up with me. I simply didn't have the opportunities to develop some of the social and sports skills the other kids had. My only option was to become the nerdy kid who walked around the playground with another nerdy kid while everyone else played baseball. I hated it!

My Grandpa was my childhood hero. He was a six–foot tall, straight standing German who served as an interpreter for the Allies in the Great War. He once met General John J. "Blackjack" Pershing, Commander of the American forces in WWI. Grandpa had time to listen to me and was tolerant of my questions. He had great stories, too. We could talk about anything as we sat in the evening shade, in those old metal lawn chairs, listening to the cicadas as they provided the soundtrack for our conversation. I still love their song.

In the summer, I would often visit my grandparents in the tiny town of Cosby, Missouri (population: 189) for days at a time. It was a good place for a kid to run around and be a little unruly and wild. My pack of young friends and I rode our bikes everywhere; down to the river, up to the ball park, to the hardware store to look at fishing gear, knives, and fireworks, and to the gas station to buy a bottle of Mason's Root Beer. Back in the day, the old men of the town always sat on a repurposed church pew there next to the pop machine. I was hemmed in everywhere else, but in Cosby, I was free to roam, pick strawberries, find adventure, and relish conversation with my Grandpa.

In high school, I struggled to find my tribe. I wasn't one of the "cool" kids who were the jocks, cheerleaders, and Student Council types. The "druggies" were out of the mainstream, but quite alluring to me. I never did drugs, but two of my more insightful friends were drug users. The "gearheads" were the guys with grease under their fingernails who were always working on their cars. The "dummies", (yes, unfortunately, that's what they were called), were the kids who didn't make it into the advanced classes. I was in the semi-cool kid's tribe, in advanced classes and with some social connections, but shy of the full popularity package of the cool kids. Honestly, I didn't know who I was. Does anyone in high school?

In these early years of my life, I fleetingly felt the confidence and direction from being connected and respected. But, what sticks with me is the loneliness of being on the outside and looking in. I was the nerdy kid who walked around the playground with the other nerdy kid while everyone else played baseball.

The Convert

I genuinely enjoyed some of my classes in high school and I admired a couple of my teachers who were passionate educators. I told people I was going to be a social studies teacher, but that whole idea was overridden by an event that forever changed my life.

When I was in elementary school, we lived close to a tiny non-denominational church. This church was so tiny; they couldn't afford a full-time pastor. My parents were Christmas and Easter churchgoers at the time, but they wanted my brother and me to have some religious influence. So, on Sunday mornings, they made sure we dressed for church and walked down the road to attend at the tiny congregation. It gave them the opportunity to sleep in and read the Sunday paper.

One Sunday, a fiery young preacher delivered a vivid sermon on Hell, a place I was sure I did not want to visit, let alone be banished to for all eternity. The preacher gave us a quick "Romans Road" explanation of salvation (explaining conversion using verses from the New Testament book of Romans) and tried to assure us of our deliverance.

I had already done the "accept Jesus as my Savior" thing, but I still had some doubts it had "taken", and I had not yet publically proclaimed my faith. That day, my gang of young church friends all walked the aisle, also, apparently, not wanting to wind up in Hell. I decided to join my friends up front. It was the perfect time to publicly proclaim my faith without complete and utter embarrassment. Still, the first step was remarkably difficult, and the church aisle seemed as long as an airport runway.

Then, something happened I will never forget. All of us young church hooligans were ushered to the front to be greeted by the big people. Darn near every person in attendance came by to shake our hands and share some words of encouragement with us. There was even an occasional hug, something less common in that day.

This deeply moved me. Tears began to roll down my face; not a good thing for an eleven-year-old boy, so I quickly wiped them away before anyone could see. Yet, I was impressed that, in a time when children had very little status, these adults would be so kind to a child like me who they hardly knew. I thought, "This is a good place."

We moved not long after, and my family went on a church hiatus for several years. My parents talked about going to a church they attended when they first married, but didn't get around to it until I was seventeen.

The Cool Dude

When I finally became involved in church again, I loved it because I was much cooler at church than I was at school. It was a smaller pond and easier to find my way to the top of the popularity food chain. I became president of the youth group, played guitar with the youth choir, and dated several of the girls in the group.

I still remember a Sunday School discussion, led by our youth pastor, about The Ten Commandments. At age seventeen, I said, "The Ten Commandments are unnecessary!" My overly dramatic youth pastor acted like I just shot him. I went on to explain how, if we followed Jesus and loved as he taught us, we wouldn't need the Ten Commandments. That would seem to mark my earliest days of being a troublemaker.

I was surprised by how many kids partied on Saturday and bragged about it when they went to church on Sunday; although, to be honest, I was one of them on occasion. The youth group was a rag tag bunch of teens who were into all the typical vices: drinking, drugs, and sex. This might be when I first began to love rag tag groups of people. We were a close group.

Unfortunately, everything they taught at this church seemed to be connected to loyalty to the church and the denomination.

The young senior pastor was jealous of the popular youth pastor. This is the same senior pastor who later warned my future in-laws about me, even though he hardly knew me. (I still really dislike the guy!) Anyway, the youth pastor threatened to "split the church right down the middle," if the senior pastor and his cronies had him kicked out.

During this upheaval, one of the youth group's sponsors (a married man with children) had an affair with a teenage girl in the youth group. This was obviously, a crime, sexual abuse, a horrible example, and seriously wrong on so many levels. They were both friends of mine and it hurt like hell when I found out. I thought, "This is not a good place."

However, two of the most important things in my life happened at that church. First, I met my wife. She says I dated all of her friends first, but that is a slight exaggeration. The second thing happened the summer between my junior and senior year in high school.

The Hippie Preacher

The local Baptist Association was celebrating its centennial. So, they did what Southern Baptists always do to mark a special occasion; they had a revival meeting. They brought in an evangelist from the Baptist Mecca of Texas and held a series of meetings at a beautiful park amphitheater in town, the same place where I graduated from High School and my wife graduated from Nurse's School.

One night, during the revival meeting, something strange happened. Some non-churched, uninitiated young adults walked in and sat down. It was the early seventies and these people looked to be (tie)dyed-in-the-wool hippies. The preacher interrupted his own sermon to welcome them as they sat down. Then and there, I had an epiphany. This situation was explosive, because three things were converging: the Good News about Jesus, a gifted messenger, and real people. It occurred to me that what the evangelist was doing was the most important job in the world. Then, out of nowhere, it hit me. I was supposed to be doing this!

That prompting felt really weird and I didn't know what to do with it. So, I ignored it, and didn't tell anyone about it.

One of the other cool things about that messed up Baptist church were the mission trips. For me, it was an opportunity to cuddle with girlfriends on long bus trips, and make new girlfriends in new towns. It was all a teenage adventure. Actually, I think the girlfriends were the adventure. One trip was more than a little awkward when a girlfriend from one town visited me in another town where I had made another girlfriend. Consumed with panic, I asked my youth pastor friend for his advice, which was, "Play it by ear, son."

As we were making the long trip back to Missouri after a mission trip to Glorietta, New Mexico, my youth pastor turned to me and asked what my plans were. I had just graduated from high school, and I had always told people my plan was to become a high school social science teacher. I had a great social science teacher, loved the field of study, and I was a bit of a nerd. So, it fit. Yet, for a full year, I had felt an unshakeable tug in my heart toward vocational ministry, initiated by my experience at the revival meeting in the park.

The youth pastor was the first person I ever said anything to about my secret calling. We talked for hundreds of miles as he drove and I sat on the warm engine cover of the old, flat-nosed school bus. I had every kind of question and concern you can think of. There were no preachers in my family. I was concerned about how my parents would react. I was troubled by my own sinfulness. I struggled with the security of my own salvation. I had questions about the educational requirements for pastors. He patiently answered my every question and concern.

Then, upon return to my hometown, I faithfully followed his recommendations. I told my parents and I made a public profession of my call into full-time Christian service. That's the way Southern Baptists do it.

Finally, it was time for my first sermon at age eighteen. My text was Matthew 12:9–14 and the title of the sermon was, "The Man with the Withered Hand." My trusty youth pastor helped me write it because I didn't know beans about writing a sermon. I remember being impressed how Jesus noticed a needy person everybody else seemed to ignore. Actually, I am still impressed by that today.

There I was, a skinny kid wearing a bright red sport coat and red and black suede shoes, with long hair and nineteenth-century length sideburns, preaching away like I knew just what I was doing.

Within a few years, I had preached at almost every little Baptist church in the region, and I wanted to pastor every one of them. I loved it. It was me! I had a huge sense of calling. For many years I struggled to gain a sense of security about my salvation, but odd as it may seem, I never doubted my pastoral calling.

My latter teen years ended in a bit of an explosion. I was devastated when my girlfriend broke up with me. The messed up Baptist church blew up when the Youth Pastor finally resigned and the church discovered the affair between the married youth group sponsor and my teenage friend. I went to a Southern Baptist College, then secretly dropped out mid-term and resumed my old job at a hardware and auto parts wholesaler. I had started to live it up, and was about to get into all sorts of trouble, when someone named Patty Spalding stole my heart. She still has it today.

We were married when she was eighteen and I was twenty. We were parents at twenty-two and twenty-four. I was horribly immature and impatient, which may explain why I had a pattern of doing things at a young age.

The early years of our marriage were consumed by both of us working our way through college, being young parents, learning how to be married, and being immersed in church activities. We high-tailed it out of the messed up church and began attending another Baptist church in town; the one all the church moths fluttered around. It was growing and exciting. The people there acted like they believed God truly heard their prayers, and there was more Bible and less church and denominational politics in the sermons and lessons.

The downside of the church was their high divorce rate. One deacon wound up marrying his best friend's (another deacon) wife. For years, the church continued to have a high divorce rate among its leadership. I don't know why; it's just an observation.

The most memorable thing about the church was the pastor. He was a career military man who had eventually retired and became a full-time pastor. He was dissed by the other Baptist pastors in the area because he didn't go to seminary. After all, he hadn't "paid his dues," yet he pastored the fastest growing church in town. He was an amazing pulpiteer who could also do a fine job of belting out a country Gospel song. He would often re-preach a published sermon and do a better job than the original preacher; sort of like when Johnny Cash would cover another musician's song. He was a charismatic leader who knew how to get things done. I admired him. I was eventually ordained as a deacon and a minister of the gospel at this happening Baptist church.

After my wife completed nursing school, I became more serious about finishing my own education. But, going to the local state college frustrated me, because I couldn't find the connection between the courses I was taking and my call into the ministry. So, I dropped out of college again.

The Bible Thumper

At some point, I heard about something called a "Bible College," which was about an hour's drive away in Kansas City. I checked it out and fell in love with it because they actually had classes on books of the Bible, areas of theology, and pastoral skills. I was like a kid in a candy store! It was another shortcut for me, because it beat the idea of going to the state college and then going to seminary. Besides, I had heard negative things about the nearest denominational seminary being "liberal" and killing true passion for ministry.

I began making the drive to attend the Bible College, even though I was the father of two and worked full-time. One semester, I ate two meals a day in the car while driving and ate the third one at work. Then I had less than an eight hour gap between work and being on the road the next day for school.

I would have momentary lapses of consciousness almost every day while making the hour-long commute, but I only had a few close calls. Before I started this commute, I could drive anywhere and not become sleepy. But, after all this driving, I couldn't be behind the wheel for fifteen minutes without fighting a major battle to stay awake. Still, I loved Bible College!

People at the college were a little suspicious of me because I was a Southern Baptist which was, believe it or not, too liberal for them. Southern Baptists were very suspicious of me because I didn't go to their seminary. The Bible College was about as fundamentalist as is possible. It was Calvinistic[1], dispensational[2], and into secondary separation, meaning they encouraged maintaining distance from other Christians who believed a little differently.

They had lots of rules, too. I didn't like them, but signed off on them to get a "good Bible education." I missed out on popular culture for a few years because there were rules prohibiting long hair, jeans, movies, theater, opera, "secret societies", rock music, and entangling alliances (whatever that is).

For me, it has always been about the calling, the vocation. My life and identity were indistinguishable from what I did. What I did was who I was. My emotions hung on tight to the roller coaster of how things were going with me and the church.

I hate to admit it, but when I think back over my life, I tend to think in terms of ministerial ups and downs instead of what was going on with my family. My lowest times have been when "my calling" was threatened, and my greatest joys were when I was in the midst of its fulfillment. I'm not proud of having felt that way, and certainly don't recommend it, but it was my reality.

Even in those early years, I became depressed by having to meet the educational requirements for vocational ministry. When I would have an opportunity to preach or be an interim pastor, I would perk up and feel alive. I was called! I knew it! I was sure of it! I loved it! Why couldn't I just jump in and begin pastoring? What's wrong with people for not giving me the opportunity? What's wrong with this screwy system and all of its requirements? That was me in all of my immaturity and impatience; I was driven to fulfill my calling. I still am.

Even though I dropped out of college twice, was married, had two children, worked full-time, drove a hundred miles round-trip to school, and sat out a few semesters, I did finally make it to graduation day with a Bachelor's degree in Pastoral Studies.

two

Dyed-in-the-Wool Insider

A few months ago I met radio Bible teacher, seminary professor, and author, Steve Brown. The first words out of his mouth were, "We have something in common. We used to be pastors. You have to be crazy to do that job!" There are, indeed a lot of crazy things about serving an evangelical church as their pastor. For one thing, you serve at the pleasure of the congregation or church leadership body; they can fire you at any time!

The most difficult thing for me was the multitude of expectations congregants had of me. Some people wanted a pastor who is personable and kind, who is good at visiting the shut-ins and people in the hospital. Some wanted a fiery preacher who will step on toes…everyone's except theirs. Some wanted a Bible scholar who serves up the Sunday sermon just so. Some wanted a miracle-working CEO who can turn a dead church around, double attendance, and triple the offering all by himself. Some wanted a friend. Some wanted a man of God who is a better role model than they ever plan on being. Some wanted a cool dude who can attract the young folks. Some wanted someone to tell them want to do. A lot of them wanted someone they could tell what to do. These people can all be in the same church!

Churches have their own personality, too, and that's where I will pick up my story.

The Church Planter

Finally, my dream came true. We moved south of Kansas City to a little bedroom town to be closer to the Bible College I was attending. In my mid-twenties, I began pastoring my first church. It was a fledgling church, or what Southern Baptists call a mission church. It had been started by one well-off and strong-minded couple who didn't like the stodgy First Baptist Church in town. However, they were the third Southern Baptist Church in the small town. One was stodgy. One was charismatic. This one was evangelistic and loving.

We met in the middle school, then in a daycare, and lastly in the elementary school. While I was with the church, we purchased a choice piece of property. The influential family who had started the church kept pressing to build a building, but the church was too small to responsibly take that step. When I left, the next pastor, who was also a banker, helped them obtain a loan for their building. It turns out he wasn't too popular. I found out years later he was jealous of me, which I found humorous and, honestly, a little gratifying.

One awesome thing about this church was the way we reached out to people on the "other side of the tracks." Actually, my little family lived on the other side of the tracks in a transient area of apartments and duplexes. Our neighbors were friendly drug dealers, who let their small children run wild throughout the neighborhood until they were called in well after dark. Usually, they gathered in our backyard and played with our kids.

The couple who started the church had a soft spot for children. So, we obtained permission to build a playground on a vacant lot across the street from our duplex so the kids would have a place to play. We bought and installed some hefty, used playground equipment and kept the lot mowed.

At one point, our thirty-something next door neighbor died of complications of HIV/AIDS acquired from doing drugs. This was the eighties, when AIDS was new and terrifying. The family asked me to have her funeral. Just after we left the area, we heard thrilling stories of how the main drug dealer (also our neighbor) had come to faith.

Those were good-hearted people at that church. They weren't very realistic, but they were good-hearted. I didn't like being subject to the every whim of the influential family and wished there were other strong leaders in the church. The little church grew, and we had quite a ministry to children, but I became restless with its smallness and limited potential. So, after four years, I looked for greener pastures.

When the church celebrated its tenth anniversary, they asked me to speak at a commemorative service in the new building their banker-pastor had helped them fund. It was the nineties, and, having strayed far from my fundamentalist and Baptist roots, I was now gung-ho on the Willow Creek seeker-service model. (Willow Creek is a megachurch in the Chicago area, whose services are huge productions geared toward the uninitiated.) A lot had changed in how I approached church, but to my utter amazement, nothing had changed at the church I had helped to begin. There were the same Sunday-dressed people with their daughters in frilly dresses, the same hymns, the same piano, the same insider talk from the pulpit. It was a time warp for me!

Much of the church lives in a time-warp, always tending to be well behind its cultural setting. Churchgoers want to hang on to things which have become precious to them; the same things that have been incorrectly identified with orthodoxy. In other words, the church is resistant to change because they like things the way they are. Often, they feel resisting change is an act of holiness and righteousness.

Fundamentalist-minded people are always looking to the past, wanting to return to the good-old-days when the church and the country stood for "Christian values." They want to "get back to the Bible." They see all of society's problems as straying away from the purity and convictions of the past. They even embrace many of the methodologies of the past, such as Sunday School and revival meetings. These things define their comfort zone and they can become pretty angry with anyone who messes with it. While resistance to change is a universal human trait, the church is an intense example of people tenaciously grasping the ways of the familiar and comfortable.

Even the contemporary church movement, with its rock bands, seeker friendliness, and polished productions has clung to those methodologies long after they have worn themselves out. There is often utter disregard for those who are disenfranchised by the prevailing church system, including entire generations of people who need a way of being the church that is real, relational, and offers a safe place to express questions and doubts. It particularly frustrates me how the church holds on to their comforting folkways solely for their own reassurance, while alienating everybody else. It seems so selfish, so uncaring, and so unlike Jesus.

The Good-Old-Boy Pastor

My pastoral wanderlust led me to a church in a city in central Illinois. It had a beautiful building in a great location, but was really just a country, good-old-boy church that happened to be in the city. The people were amazingly loving, congenial, and kind, and I became well connected in the city. We loved it there!

You knew there was an "except" coming, didn't you?

These wonderful folks just wanted someone to preach with passion who would visit the sick, the shut-ins, and occasionally, the other congregants. Things rolled along just fine... until I realized my little kingdom didn't look anything like The Church in Acts 2. Then, I made things worse by reading George Barna[1] books. He confirmed my suspicions; the church was stuck in the fifties. With their love of Southern Country Gospel quartets and pot-luck suppers, this church was really stuck in the fifties.

I could do most anything I wanted as long as it didn't bother them or require much of them. I siphoned some of my energy into community ministries and led the local CareNet Pregnancy Center Board and the local ministerial association. I soon found more fulfillment in community activities than in trying to lead my own church. I have always been more successful working with a diverse team in community-wide organizations. These organizations prospered, and I felt fulfilled in that role, but I struggled with the pervasive inertia in my church.

While serving the good-old-boy church in central Illinois, I learned the local black pastors association was trying to rewrite their constitution and by-laws. I had just written the constitution and by-laws for the ministerial association. So, I was familiar with the process and offered to help. I walked into their meeting as the lone white face and was graciously accepted. As I listened to their conversations, I soon found out they were Democrats. I was so steeped in the conservative white Evangelical culture of the eighties that I couldn't understand how a Christian, let alone a pastor, could possibly be a Democrat. For one thing, at that time the abortion controversy was front-and-center in Evangelical politics, and most Democrats were not pro-life, while Evangelicals were overwhelmingly pro-life and Republican.

I helped write their constitution and made a friend along the way, the first black friend I ever had. I remember having lunch with him and talking frankly about racial issues. He said it all comes down to relationships and knowing people as individuals. He was right! When we know individuals, we can't conveniently bunch people together and use the pronouns, "they" and "them."

About that time, the Rodney King verdict was handed down, and people all over America feared a violent reaction, which indeed happened. Our city was a backward place where racial attitudes seemed to lag behind the social norm. So, we also feared a violent response locally. The evangelical pastors were in a meeting when the news of the verdict broke. Because we now had some relationships in the black pastoral community, we were able to quickly meet together for a time of prayer in the central park of the city. That was one of the few times I was ever on TV. It was an awesome moment and a good visual for the city; black men and white men holding hands and praying their hearts out for the same thing.

The church I was pastoring was so into its own sub-culture it was not even in tune with the rest of Evangelicalism. Therefore, they thought I was a little weird for making such a big deal about abortion and race relations, even though these were Evangelical hot button issues of the day.

One Sunday morning there was an ominous sounding knock at my office door. It was the chairman of the church board who looked rather somber. It was obvious he was bearing some sort of bad news. He explained I had done something that did not set at all well with the congregation and my leadership was being called into question. What was the infraction, you might ask? I had changed the order of the Sunday morning service and moved the offering to the end of the service. This incident was, unfortunately, a true indicator of the depth of the vision of this church. Realizing it wasn't a significant issue one way or the other, I moved the offertory back to the traditional spot in the order of service. Geesh!

I had a long honeymoon that lasted two years into a six-year tenure. A few things happened, like the above incident, which caused me to realize my congregation and I had drastically different values, and this revelation threw me into a significant depression!

I started considering my options. Could I change the prevailing mindset? Did I want to make an extremely long-term commitment to a church with little hope of being vital during the next ten or twenty years? What had I done by moving my family there? Do I now uproot my wife from a job she loves, my kids from their school and their friends, and myself from my friends and connections throughout the community to move on to something else? I felt trapped and demoralized. That's why I found more enjoyment in my community involvement than I did from pastoring the church.

Believe me, there are numerous pastors who feel trapped. They may not feel optimistic about their church's prospects. They may have had it with all of the crazy expectations congregants place on them. They may have become addicted to the adrenaline rush of responding to every whim of their members and being the go-to guy. They may be exhausted by their compulsion to please people. But, it is hard to leave a stable job with a decent salary, benefits, and a retirement plan, with no clue about how you would make a living.

Deciding what to do became an area of conflict in our marriage. I was ready to flee. My wife was not. My kids were not. So, I served for three more years after I realized this church was a dead end. I had to tread water as an idealist in a self-satisfied church. Finally, I began to put out feelers for another church. It was yet another year before we moved on. That was a long time to feel trapped!

The Transition Leader

The last church I pastored was in a large, aging Chicago suburb. Coming to the Chicago area was a culture shock for us. People took themselves way more seriously and were more focused on being correct than being congenial. The church was one of those super-serious Bible teaching churches that always had several seminary students in attendance.

I had been looking for more serious-minded leadership and I found it. They were so serious, they were paralyzed. The church had been divided between the older fundamentalists and the middle-aged Evangelicals for several years. Efforts to find a common direction had been to no avail. They were also an Anglo island in a primarily Hispanic city, and their numbers had been shrinking for several years. Then, I walked in the door, all culture-shocked and trying to figure out how to hit the ball in a new ballpark.

Of course, I adjusted to the local culture and even began driving like the people in Chicago. But I knew we needed more of a focus to move the church forward and the stress between the two groups continued to grow. After a couple of years of trying to make it work, the solution came to me like an epiphany (yep, another one). This common direction is not something to be decided by us. It was already given to us; it is essentially the Great Commandment (make disciples of all people) and The Great Commission (love God and love your neighbor.)

I simply said we would evaluate everything we did in light of the mission already given to us. People could see it would mean change and they felt threatened by it. Ironically, both factions united in questioning my leadership. I knew it would be a rough road, but I pressed on. Relationships became even more strained, and the church became a tense place. After a great deal of grief and in spite of many meetings and conversations, families began to leave one-by-one. After a while, only a handful of people were left. I had never been part of anything like this before. The people who left knew their church would become so different it wouldn't seem like their church anymore. That is, in fact, exactly what happened.

One time, a prominent older gentleman told me I should listen to some recordings of a previous pastor in order to learn how to preach a proper expository sermon. (Have you ever tried to find an expository sermon preached by Jesus, Paul, or anyone else in the Bible?) It was his way of telling me he didn't care for the way I was serving up his weekly bit of biblical inspiration. It was demoralizing to hear comments like that after I had poured out my heart and soul in days of prayer and study. I didn't listen to the recommended recordings because I didn't care to be somebody else. Besides, I had a strong sense the complainer was a finicky consumer.

Another time, we removed the wrap-around pulpit and replaced it with a simple wooden stand because there had been a skit on the stage. The same gentleman made certain the big ugly pulpit was moved back before the next service began, as though the furniture on the stage was incredibly important. He always told the sound guy to turn the volume down, and I always told him to turn it up.

This gentleman's proper wife was so ashamed her granddaughter had been born before her mom was married that she didn't tell anyone about her new grandbaby. I find it sickening, as I think how pride can get in the way of love and how unlike Jesus we can become in the name of "righteousness." To give her the benefit of the doubt, maybe she feared the judgment of others in the church. In any case, it is a sad way to respond to the birth of a baby in your family.

I remember an anonymous letter in which its mean-spirited and cowardly author recounted some illustrations I had used in recent sermons. The author indicated that he only wanted to hear the Bible in sermons. During my years in the pastorate, I heard complaints about almost everything imaginable, but this was my first anti-illustration complaint.

One of our elders was a serious-minded young man. He and his family had left the church, but he showed up on AWANA (a midweek children's program) night to talk to me. He started out with, "Do you know what you have done to this church?" Then, he recited the names of some people who had left the church. For the next two hours he told me everything he thought was wrong with me and described how I had destroyed his church.

While he was talking, I silently prayed, trying to figure out how to respond. I felt the best thing to do was to say nothing, except to agree with him when he was right, and he was right about a few things. I wasn't as in-touch with the children's programs as I should have been and I certainly hadn't handled all of the trauma and transition this church had gone through perfectly. I let him talk until he ran out of steam and then asked him about his family and prayed with him.

One day, I picked up a magazine published by the denomination of the church this serious-minded elder had migrated to. Within its pages, he was quoted as saying how the pastor at his new church was so wonderful. The pastor's communication style connected with him and he loved the changes he was making. Ironically, when I had made these same types of changes at the church I was pastoring (this man's previous church); he seemed to think these changes had "destroyed" his church.

Once the naysayers were gone, I was left with a tiny group of supportive people who had either come into the church on my watch, had stayed out of the fray all together, or else, they just liked me. We all felt a sense of relief in our new freedom to move forward as we began to create a different church. Our finances were, of course, severely curtailed, but something happened I had never heard of before. For two years, another local church of a different stripe supplemented my salary, ensuring that I could continue full-time with the church.

We re-wrote our constitution, remodeled our dated building, and re-worked our ministries. We reduced our programs down to Sunday services and small groups. In the great exodus, we had lost almost all of our musicians. So, I began to pray we would be blessed with musical individuals and in a few months, we were inundated with musicians. We transitioned from organ and piano to one of the rockin'-est churches around. Spontaneous ministry was happening like crazy through the small groups and people became close with one another. We were finally experiencing the re-birth I had dreamed of. I loved it.

We were no longer the super serious, stodgy old Bible church. We had become a down-and-outers church with a contemporary flair. We did spontaneous acts of kindness, like a free carwash, giving away bottles of water and Pepsi at ball games, paying peoples' tolls on the toll way, and having a neighborhood dinner for the business owners in our area. Still, we didn't grow much and we were, more than ever, an Anglo island in the heart of Little Mexico. However, for years we hosted a Hispanic congregation which grew like crazy.

We had a lot of artists, especially musicians, and we were convinced to stay with a trendy, seeker-oriented service. Eventually, we began to think about moving, and we easily sold our building to a black congregation whose pastor was a good friend of mine.

Many of my closest friends were black or Hispanic and many of them were of the Charismatic persuasion. One black pastor and I had a sibling-like relationship; we preached at each other's churches, and we were well known throughout each other's congregations, which were almost like sister churches. That was a rewarding contrast to my past.

Upon selling our building, we rented office space and a movie theater in the neighboring, more affluent suburbs. We didn't want to turn our back on the aging, mostly Hispanic city; we just didn't know how to reach the people there any better than the Hispanic Church which was already there.

We were a rag-tag group of people that included a few drug addicts, but we loved each other. We did lose a few people in the move. I think it was a stretch for everyone to become a part of a labor-intensive, church-in-the-box operation. Being a seeker-friendly, high-tech church that met in a movie theater meant we had tons of equipment to set up and take down every Sunday. In retrospect, I regret how we followed the advice of some of our more yuppyish members by cleaning up and polishing our act for the suburbanites, losing too much of our authenticity and uniqueness in the process. So, our move was a little bit shaky. Actually, it was much shakier than I realized.

A seminary professor and author attended our church, and he usually showered me with reassuring accolades. However, one time, we were in a meeting with some key people to discuss the possibly of making the move to the burbs. A friend of mine on staff at Willow Creek Community Church (a Chicago area megachurch) was also there to help us sort through the issues involved and offer his opinion. The meeting went long, and eventually just three of us were left. I spoke my mind about making the move. How the seminary professor responded shocked me and the other person present.

He said it concerned him that I was making all of the decisions. His words were more than a little surprising. Believe me; I had taken everything step-by-step, in order to move forward in a unified fashion. Somehow, without warning, I went from being the best pastor around to being dictatorial and of grave concern to this learned man. I met with him to talk it out. He informed me he was moving and would be attending another church where some of his other seminary buddies attended. I felt like I needed him at the juncture we were in, but his mind was made up.

His son was our worship leader. (Can you see it coming?) He and his wife were becoming disenchanted about something neither my wife nor I can remember these eleven years later. I find it kind of ironic that this guy and his wife destroyed a fledgling church over something we can't remember. I do remember when I brought it up to other people; they didn't get it either. Anyway, they were dragging their feet on the move.

I didn't know until later that his dad (the seminary professor) talked with him regularly about our church, stirring him up more with each conversation. Of course, the worship leader was someone I had poured a lot into and had met with him one-on-one every week for at least a year. After the move was put in motion, I began to see it as a gigantic risk, given how shaky things were. But, it was too late to change our plans because the building had already been sold.

Several things happened to delay our launch in the theater, moving it into the holiday season. We classed up our act for the suburbanites, did our mass mailing, and attracted a few new people.

Yet, all the while the undercurrent created by the disgruntled family was stronger than I realized. We were essentially falling apart while we were trying to launch. The atmosphere with the family had become toxic and strained as they deliberately and aggressively spread their message of discontent, trying to recruit people to their way of seeing things. People began leaving until our ability to continue on in that setting which required so much manpower and commitment became impossible.

Near my birthday, in February, I remember the palatable sense of stress that came with putting on a service. Even the normal routine was hard enough. I started at 5:00 AM, first by reviewing the sermon and the service, and then getting ready, opening up the theater, setting up, cleaning up again in the theater restroom, praying with service participants, trying to keep everyone pumped up, doing the service, schmoozing with the visitors, helping the take-down/clean-up crew, and falling asleep while eating my lunch.

That Sunday in February, I remember the stark realization that my dream had turned into a nightmare. I walked down a deserted hall to some of the other theaters in the multiplex which was still closed to the public at that hour, looked out the exterior door at the cold, snowy scene outdoors, and wondered in disbelief at what had happened. This was the dream that had led me to move my family all around the Midwest. This was the dream that I had paid for with ten years of patient transition with an unlikely church. This was the dream that I had been maligned for by cranky, entrenched, hard core church members. Now, my dream had turned into a nightmare, and I didn't even want to be there!

Eventually, enough people left that we could not sustain a quality service. A couple of dozen people stayed with us as we moved into my family room and did a home Bible study. These folks were the faithful of the faithful. I took a church planting course and we made an attempt at a re-launch of the church by putting up posters and holding an informational meeting. I felt this was the last ditch effort. If God wanted a church there, the people would come. Otherwise, it was time to close it down.

On the appointed day of the re-launch meeting, only a couple of new people came. I remember the sickening feeling of going through the motions of explaining the vision of the new church that obviously was not going to happen. That was just before we left to visit our families in Missouri at Thanksgiving. My heart was broken.

Eventually, we decided to disband the church and help out some missionaries and local churches with our finances from selling the church building and by donating all our new equipment. I sadly packed my office, full of two decades worth of books and mementos, to move to my home. We employed an attorney and did everything by the book as we dissolved the church. I didn't even take a paper clip home that had been purchased with church funds. It was a bitter pill and painful to explain to people, although I became pretty good at explaining it, and had a long and short version of our sad story.

Several months after the dissolution, I received a notice from the Illinois Secretary of State informing me the dissolution process was being investigated to determine how we disbursed our considerable financial resources. I was thankful everything was carefully documented and as legal as we knew to make it. Thanks to the good work of my administrative assistant, we furnished every document requested and were cleared of any wrongdoing. One of the disgruntled church members had initiated the investigation.

When the church was still meeting in my family room, I received an email from a former member encouraging me to give all of the church's money to one particular missionary. The crazy thing was I didn't even know the guy. His membership predated my ten years there. Upon advice from those church members who were left, I politely let this guy know that he had absolutely no say in what we do with anything.

It was just another bit of evidence of the arrogance and selfish type of ownership some people possessed in this particular church. It was one heck of a ride, to say the least!

I was a churchman to the core. I loved the church. I studied the church and kept up with the latest trends. I was critical of those who were not deeply involved in a local church. The "insider" tag definitely fit me to a "T."

Granted, what I have told you about my church experience has been mostly the negative stuff, because it explains my drift toward an irreligious faith. I learned how churches have leaders other than the staff and how churches have a personality that is devilishly difficult to change.

But, all was not negative. I made many wonderful friends. Some have endured all the turmoil and are still friends after all these years. I had the joy of feeling totally alive doing what I felt called to do. I enjoyed the honor being present at key moments in peoples' lives. I loved having a strong sense of calling and feeling passionate about what I was doing.

Overall, I both loved and disliked being a pastor. I loved being the go-to-guy. It fit the needs of my ego and personality. I liked being needed by needy people. It was a symbiotic relationship that fed my own neediness. I enjoyed the challenge of creative communication. However, I was never favorably inclined toward the more formal pastoral responsibilities, like officiating at funerals and weddings. I just am not a formal sort of guy.

I was frustrated by the vast and unreasonable array of expectations placed on me as a pastor by congregants. I was always bothered by the self-centeredness I encountered within the church, which made everything subject to the desires and whims of the congregants with no consideration for the uninitiated.

three

Idealistic Reformer

When the church closed, I intended to take a little time to decompress and do some of the odd jobs around the house I had deferred because I was always busy with pastor stuff. I organized everything in the house, threw out bunches of stuff, re-roofed the house and garage, put on new storm doors, and the like.

I always thought I would find another pastor gig. Even with all I had been through, I was still in love with the church and married to my calling. Also, I was always connected with other pastors and usually wound up heading up community ministries. I was the president of the CareNet Pregnancy Center Board and two different local ministers' associations, as well as the county chairman of a host of events with the international evangelist Luis Palau.

I thought some of my pastor friends would invite me to pinch hit for services or help out in some capacity, since I often would turn to other pastors. Instead, it was as though I had died. Nobody in the local pastoral or Christian community reached out to me. Nobody!

I was no longer affiliated with a denomination. I had just closed a church. I was confined to the area because my wife had a good job we could not afford to leave, unless I was called by a large church. I had to stay nearby. In other words, I was screwed and I was alone.

I had some interviews. A couple of them were on site at prospective churches. But, I soon found out that churches were either looking for a "Superstar" who could single-handedly double the attendance and triple the offering, or a "Brother Bud" who would be content to keep the sheep happy who were already in the fold. I had no aspirations of becoming either sorry character.

For over ten years, I have been unemployed, under-employed, or mis-employed. I have washed windows, sold cars, run my own window cleaning and painting company, and worked as an account executive for a high tech company. I hated every one of these jobs, except when my son would help me on painting jobs. Finally, I embarked upon an extensive course of study in nonprofit management, which I enjoyed, but I was not able to land a job in the field. I worked for two years as a volunteer with a coalition of community leaders to help them develop an advocacy organization, only to become totally disillusioned by their lack of vision and leadership.

The Church Hopper

It was several years after my transition from pastor to congregant before I even thought about not attending church. I had hoped to have some influence in a church, while still being careful to be supportive of the staff. After all, I knew what betrayal felt like and saw how destructive it can be.

Over the course of eight years or so, we attended three conventional churches and two house churches. This was all new to me, having never been a church shopper or church hopper.

For about three months, we went to a young church led by an exceptional musician and preacher. We had given that church all of our equipment and several thousand dollars when we dissolved. I offered to help out however I could, but they made it clear they already had their pastor. This guy was a superstar in his church. Without a doubt, he was gifted in his role on the platform, but the church had the mentality that there can be only one go-to-guy. Sometimes, there is a tribal church mentality, and the tribe likes a chief they can admire. If he slips up, the tribe can oust him. Having never felt welcomed, we bowed out of attending this church.

It was an abrupt separation. The associate pastor was a bit caustic, in stark contrast to the lead pastor who had a pleasant spirit. He sent me a terse email stating there was no place for me in leadership and people were suspicious as to why I wanted to help out. That was the final straw, because my motives were pure. I had offered to assist, without pay, two staff members who had known me for some time and were always talking about how busy they were. I unloaded my frustration and sense of scorn in an email response. (Note to self: email is not the best way to handle issues like this.) The Lead Pastor contacted me to try to make things right. The Associate never did, so I contacted him and we talked things out. Some of my ruffled feathers were smoothed out, but there was still, no way I wanted to be a part of what they had going!

Strangely, we had repeated difficulty with them not assuming the rent for the storage space where all of the equipment we had given them was stored. It was an ongoing hassle. There was a surprising lack of gratitude from both congregations we had blessed with significant sums of money. I don't even know what that was about; just being self-consumed, I guess.

We learned of a new church a few miles away that sounded like they might be breaking the church cookie cutter mold. So, we paid them a visit. Again, it was led by a pastoral staff of two; a humorous and resourceful assistant pastor and sweet-spirited lead pastor who was an outstanding preacher. The lead pastor and I had some terrific conversations over lunch and I wound up leading their welcoming ministry and conducting a focus group study about how the church assimilated new people.

The pastor humored me when I talked about new ideas for small groups, but decided not to change their structure. As the church grew, it lost its edge and became more like every other suburban church plant. That just wasn't who we are. However, this was our best church experience after leaving the pastorate and the pastor was the best leader and preacher I encountered while trying to find a church where we could fit in and make a contribution.

The last conventional church we attended was nearby. It was the largest and trendiest of the ones we tried. The senior pastor was a kind and gentle older man who reminded us of my wife's favorite uncle. He was not a particularly talented preacher, but the services were contemporary and splashy. I liked the way the church used their building for all manner of activities and was flexible in changing and beginning new ministries. In fact, overly so. It seemed they followed every trend that came along if it was promoted by an influential megachurch.

I became quite involved, helping with the food pantry, leading their welcoming ministry, and coordinating a huge community wide festival of kindness. The event involved ten churches, five hundred volunteers, a social services expo, and the giving away of two truckloads of food. As we attempted to make it an annual event, the church staff made it clear they were significantly decreasing their involvement and financial support.

I still remember that meeting. It consisted of the Senior Pastor, the Associate Pastor, the new Executive Pastor, and me. They made it clear they were withdrawing from their previous level of commitment in reaching out to the poor. The festival of kindness was now without an anchor church, but more disappointing was the attitude they conveyed which turned me off completely. They were looking for any way they could find to put their financial house in order, with little creative thought about how to continue to reach out to the poor among them. I knew I would be a hypocrite if I continued to attend this church, so I parted ways as amicably as possible.

The Weird Guy

About this time, I did two pretty weird things. I fasted for one year; both from reading the Bible and from church attendance. I had hardly missed a day of reading the Bible in over 25 years; however, it was losing its meaning. I was reading it out of duty. The text was usually familiar. The words rolled off of my soul, making zero impact. Maybe this is what happens when you devote your life to reading, studying, and teaching, as opposed to living and loving.

I am happy to report that nothing terrible happened as a result. There were no lightning strikes, there was no backsliding (well, no more than usual), and there was no tumbling down the slippery slope of unbelief.

The problem is not knowing; the problem is living. That explains how people can know the Bible but still be such jerks. I know plenty about the Bible, maybe, too much. I have accountability for that knowledge to work its way into my life, and that's what I tried to focus on during my fast.

At the conclusion of my Bible fast, I did something else pretty weird. I determined to read one book of the Bible very slowly. I also determined not to bog down in scholarly research as I read. One last thing, I decided to write about it on my blog. It took about a year to read and write my way through John's Gospel. I wanted to understand it, communicate it in practical terms, and try to picture what it would be like if Jesus were doing those things today. This was a great experience. I was struck by how revolutionary and counter cultural Jesus was.

As I mentioned, I also fasted from church attendance for one year. This was unusual for me because I was always such a church lover. In the past, I would even find a church to attend when traveling and while on vacation. But, it was also becoming less meaningful to me. I needed to cleanse my spiritual palate and assume some responsibility for my own spiritual welfare. After all those years of attending church, it felt bizarre at first. Then, it actually started feeling good.

At last, I had a true Sabbath. On Sunday, I would read and write my way through the book of John. Sometimes, Patty and I would go for walks or visit outdoor festivals. During football season, we would watch our beloved Kansas City Chiefs (and sometimes it takes a diehard fan to watch them) at our son's house, since he had the DIRECTV Sunday Ticket and a large HDTV. We pooled culinary skills and food to enjoy our own little fan cave feast. We were building relationships, sharing a meal, and being refreshed. Maybe this was more true church than church!

I recommend these fasts, odd as they sound. It is a valid way to find a faith that is real by trying to live out what we have been reading in words printed on a page and listening to preached from a platform.

I have often wondered what would happen if we showed up one Sunday to find the church building had been confiscated by the government and the pastor had been imprisoned. What would we have without our Sunday morning show and our professional clergy? What would we do?

I think most churches would get together and try to figure out how to build a building and hire a pastor. But, what if that were out of the question? The result could be something real and meaningful. We would be forced to assume responsibility for our own lives and faith. Our sense of community and mission would be blended together with regular life into a cocktail of faith and reality.

One of the best things we did during this period was to invite a bunch of young adults into our home on a weekly basis. Several of them partied hard at the time. Our little gatherings of food and discussion must have seemed incredibly lame to them, but I think everyone felt loved and accepted. One particularly outgoing member of the group, who had tremendous potential, is now dead. He aspirated on his own vomit after a night of partying. Anyway, we would feed them; that's Patty's thing, and she is incredibly good at it. Then, we would talk about whatever. It was full of meaning, but hard to keep going for very long.

For about three years, we were a part of two different house churches. They had their moments, but both are long since gone. One consisted of family members and friends who had all left the same church who would get together to watch videos by Rob Bell (a popular preacher and former pastor of a church in Grand Rapids, Michigan). The other one had some meaningful conversations but was, in fact, nothing more than a discussion group.

House churches don't seem to have much of a life span. I think they eventually become a lot like the conventional church they are protesting.

For me, discussion and community are keys to being the church. Preaching and teaching have their place, but they are way overrated. Sometimes these house churches had engaging discussions, but it seems like community was always lacking.

How do you teach somebody to live like Jesus? You walk with them. You face struggles together. You seize teachable moments. That's the Jesus way. You don't have another class!

It's a messy process, and few are willing to abandon the easy route of having a "class or small group for that."

One of the most awkward feelings ever is meeting together regularly with people who otherwise have little connection with one another. It's stressful. Unfortunately, that is the typical church approach to small groups. I know we need to grow up and not expect everybody to care deeply about us. We also need to learn to care about people we might not otherwise connect with. Yet, there has to be a normal way for people to experience community. Why can't church simply be friends getting together talking about how to live life in the way of Jesus?

The Troublemaker

So, I had become a church hopper, something I disdained as a pastor! During those years of church hopping, we stayed at each church for a few months to a few years. I still can't believe how disappointing this process was. I was idealistic about the church; I thought all church leaders shared my values.

Sometimes the churches were doing some great things, but I was restricted from being involved in a way that was true to who I am. Usually, they wanted me to "pay my dues," but I felt I had already done that and had the scars to prove it.

They wanted me to come up through the ranks all over again in their particular church. I was not willing to that. It was like being sent back to first grade after completing graduate school. I found it to be a foolish, controlling, insensitive, and myopic way to build leadership

I couldn't find a place to belong in the organization I had devoted my life to serving! Although I had experienced some hard knocks as a pastor, I wasn't ready to lay down and die! My goal was simple. The church needed some help, so I would tactfully try to suggest some ideas to help it be better.

In hindsight, I believe I saw the church as it truly is for the first time in my life.

What I encountered ran the spectrum from being humored to being flat out rejected and branded a troublemaker. That reaction surprised me. I felt I should have some credibility since I was a seasoned practitioner who had "been there and done that."

While looking for a job, I applied to a local Christian charitable organization. I knew the director, who was a former pastor, who, like me, who had closed his church. It wasn't a good job, but it did sound interesting and I was trying to get things moving any way I could.

I dressed up and went to the interview. The guy proceeded to tell me how wonderful the agency was and how God was moving through their work. He asked me where I was going to church and I told him I was attending a house church. He replied that I would need to be attending an established church to be considered for the position. There had to be a name of an established church to put beside my name on the stationary.

He went on to say he had heard I had been writing some negative things about the church on a blog. It didn't sound like he had troubled himself to read the "negative things" I had written. In fact, I am almost certain he knew I was attending a house church before he interviewed me! What was that about? It seemed to be some sort of power play to embarrass me.

Needless to say, I couldn't sit there and smile. I asked him why he wanted to exclude so many people who loved Jesus from involvement in his organization. That's when the interview became confrontational. I went looking for a job and wound up having to defend my position. The dude kept waxing eloquent about how he was on a mission from God. Then, at the end, he had the nerve to stick his hand in my face and say, "Still Friends?" Needless to say, if I had a Christmas card list, his name would not be on it.

People who are in the system can only hear so much that does not align with their paradigm. They have too much vested interest to be adventurous. Their paycheck and retirement fund could be jeopardized. Maybe God has called some people to be reformers, but not me. It is too slow, too painful, and too frustrating!

four

Confirmed Outsider

My vocation, my personal identity, and the church have always been intertwined. I finally came to the realization that, somehow, these things had to be unwound. Being my vocation was just too painful. My emotions, my sense of worth, and wellbeing would rise and fall like the tide. My happiness depended on how things were going between me and the church. I loved it, devoted my life to it, studied it, was fascinated by it, and defended it. But, it spurned my advances and rejected me, leaving me cold and lost.

I spent thousands of dollars on an education that was only good for being a pastor and quite useless in finding any other sort of job. I had been taught about the importance of doctrinal purity; something that didn't matter to people in the real world. I had decades of valuable experience that those outside the church completely disregarded. A mutiny by well-meaning, but mixed-up people took me and an entire church down. My ideas for improvements in the church were only accepted as far as they fit into the existing structures, and I always saw beyond those structures.

I still loved the church deeply, yet I had been branded a troublemaker; someone angry at the church, someone who had some bad experiences and was now just a pissed off dude trying to make his case.

My journey took me places I never dreamed, caused me to ask questions I had never thought of before, and led me to change my perspective on church and even my theology. Sometimes, I wished it had never happened because my life was so much simpler before.

Just a couple of years ago, it occurred to me that I was like a bird who had been set free from his cage, yet refused to fly around the house and out the open door into the wild and the beautiful unknown. Instead, I kept trying to get back into the cage. The cage was the institutional church or conventional expressions of the church.

I wanted church leaders to listen to me. I wanted them to care about all those people who felt disenfranchised by what should be the most accepting community on earth. I wanted them to make the necessary adjustments so the church could recapture a place of relevance in the culture. My ideas were full of common sense and were always sparingly shared in ways that were respectful of church leadership, but I never could get very far as a reformer.

Eventually, I became an outsider; because I couldn't find a church I wanted to have anything to do with and I knew I would be a huge hypocrite to attend.

Church seemed like a rather silly game. It involves spending hundreds of thousands of dollars to hire professionals. It builds buildings dedicated to insider purposes that are used only a few hours a week. It centers on a pep rally, designed to help you feel happy about your relationship with God, feel guilty about falling short of his standard, or motivate you to get involved in supporting and giving money to the organization. The presentation is the central focus and it is carefully crafted to illicit a desired response. The goals are to involve you in programs and classes to help you learn how to be a better church member and to convince you to participate in activities that would help to maintain or build the church organization.

I used to feel rather indignant when I was preaching and would look out on the congregation to find someone dozing. Without specifically pointing them out, I would try to wake them up by raising my voice. Of course, I would also note their lack of spirituality. In our latter times of church attendance, I found myself doodling, and yes, occasionally nodding off during a boring sermon.

The Spiritual Adolescent

Church just didn't connect with me anymore. I felt like I had outgrown it, and I was looking for something more real. When I met Steve Brown, he asked me what I was doing for church and I replied, "Nothing," and he warned me about appearing self-righteous. Steve is a fabulous guy and a gracious champion of grace. He was right, too. When I say I feel like I have outgrown conventional church, it can sound awfully darn self-righteous.

I never anticipated that I would choose not to be involved in a local church. It just happened. If I wasn't forced to stand back and look at the church objectively, I would love it exactly the same way I always have.

Hopefully, I can explain why my perspective toward church has changed. Please bear with me as I try to draw a parallel.

When I was a kid, I was compliant. I did what my parents said. I seldom questioned their instructions. When I did, I was told in no uncertain terms to do as I was told and to not question their authority. As I grew into a teenager, new thoughts entered my mind. I decided my parents were probably wrong about some things. I knew I wanted to try things they had forbidden and I had both the inclination and ability to do so. All

I needed was the opportunity. I could sneak around and do whatever I wanted.

I smoked for months before my parents knew, dropped out of college weeks before they knew, and went to parties they never did find out about. I also, questioned the values I had been taught. For example, I felt my parents were too materialistic. As a result, I wasn't too worried about getting my personal finances in order and I would willingly give things away to my friends. This is an example of normal adolescent development.

Kids test their parent's values, do some stupid things, and then usually wind up embracing a set of values very similar to those of their parents. It's a necessary part of growing up. We all need to grow into our own life and not just mimic what we have been taught.

I have always wondered about the parents with perfect kids. Honestly, it freaks me out because it is so unnatural and abnormal to have "perfect" kids.

Maybe...

- The parents are blissfully ignorant of their kids' real lives.
- The kids are incredibly sneaky and are stellar actors.
- The exceptionally compliant youngsters are in for real trouble later in life because they missed a normal stage of development.

Perhaps these compliant kids grow up being tremendous people-pleasers, while they are secretly seething with discontent. Maybe, their lack of normal teenage rebellion causes that rebellion to happen later, when life is much more complicated and the consequences are likely to be much more severe. Maybe, they go through life like zombies. I don't know, but deferring the processes of maturing and learning to think for yourself is abnormal.

Now, to my point. I was forced into religious adolescence. I was pushed out of the church system by events I didn't bargain for. I didn't want to grow up and would have preferred to remain the accepting, compliant child. But, when I was forced into adolescence, I took a fresh look at church. I tested the things I was taught and found a lot of stuff I didn't like. I found things that were not well-anchored in Jesus, truth, or my experience. I found new avenues of expression I felt were truer to the way of Jesus and did not rely on worn-out institutional systems.

Questioning authority is good. Questioning our governmental authorities is an important part of the foundation of our nation. Yet, when we think critically about the church, we are told it is sacrosanct. I am not talking about The Church. I am talking about the church, i.e., how we do church.

As I was forced out and began to look at the church more objectively, I found current expressions of church just weren't cutting it for me anymore. I questioned religious leaders and church practices, and came to some new conclusions.

The Companion on the Journey

I thought I was all alone in my surprising, unpredictable journey, and I felt weird as I watched the multitudes who still loved their church. It seemed as though there was something wrong with me. My feelings of loneliness and weirdness caused me to look for other people who felt the way I did. That drove me to the Internet, where I found a whole flock of people who were in the process of healing from painful church experiences and were trying to forge a faith that was real to them. When I began searching about six years ago, the interwebs were abuzz with stories of pain, coupled with a developing narrative theology[1] and new hope for the old institution. The buzz words in those days were deconstruction, conversation, and the emerging church.

I joined with these fellow travelers to try to find a new, stripped down, totally real faith I could live with. Eventually, I began a blog. Then I began Communitas Collective[2], featuring articles by a group of writers from around the world who were deconstructing and re-constructing their faith. Later Communitas became a podcast where good buddy Erik Guzman, a.k.a. The Merry Monk of Love, and I chatted with other people on the journey.

It is interesting to see what happened to those fellow journeyers. A few house churches were birthed to live meaningful, but short lives. A few churches for young adults and artsy types have been strategically planted and have done alright. Some notable exceptions have flourished. I have had the pleasure of attending Jacob's Well in Kansas City, Missouri and Solomon's Porch in Minneapolis.

Both had a hip, but ancient, feel. Solomon's porch was like having church in a used furniture store, with Pastor Doug Paggitt spinning on his barstool in order to gain momentary eye-contact with the attendees at his church-in-the-round. I remember the open discussion after the sermon in which a young adult asked for mentoring help, especially related to sex and finances. I love honesty like that!

Jacob's Well was the only place where I heard a worship song with the word "frickin'" in it. Again, a little honesty is a beautiful (and powerful) thing!

One of the problems with new, successful churches is that they often become much like what they are rebelling against. When you draw a crowd, you have to figure some things out, like what to do about the children, what kind of authority structure are you going to have, how to handle the money, how to pay staff, and how to manage the church property.

Based on my anecdotal evidence, a lot of the hope for the church was not realized. Most new churches died. The ones that survived had those pesky issues of "success" to deal with, which made them seem something like the church they left.

A lot of the people re-evaluating their church involvement and their faith became lonely and they went back into a conventional church. Some young parents wanted something religious for their children, so they went back for the sake of their kids. Some questioned their theology all the way to agnosticism or atheism. A lot of people just decided to stay out and sort of do church on the fly by enjoying God at work wherever and however it happened. Some found a new hobby and immersed themselves into the community that sprung up around it.

Pulling out of heavy involvement in church alters the rhythms and relationships of our life and usually leaves us with a lot of wounds and a major void crying out to be filled by something.

I developed an interest in nonprofit management and poverty alleviation, taking several courses on both, and began working with a community coalition. My writing interests, which were once all about the ills of the church and deconstructing and reconstructing my faith, now include most anything. I began to appreciate the challenge of writing about something I would not normally address.

The Pissed-off Old Guy

I began to note the things in life that made me angry. Anger can be instructive, and even positive, if we let our indignation point us to things we care deeply about and we begin to focus on how to make them better.

As the legal guardian for my disabled brother, I had to fight a giant corporation to get him things that were rightfully his, like retiree medical insurance. I know what it is to be locked into a battle spanning months and years with countless phone calls and emails. I saw how corporations outsource benefits administration. I have dealt with under-empowered, under-paid customer service representatives who cannot even find The Letter of Guardianship I faxed to them six years ago. Some companies seem to purposefully leave you with no reasonable recourse.

Customer service, in general, is laughable. The representatives have to try to handle complex complaints while being undertrained and underpaid. Companies seem content to part ways with their customers rather than provide decent customer service.

I learned that social services are program-centered rather than people-centered and are built around providing services rather than partnering with people to achieve their goals. They are so fragmented; almost no one knows how to successfully navigate all available services.

Education is prohibitively expensive, as you progress through a long list of non-job-related requirements that someone decided are part of a "well-rounded education." Formal education is also not always so great at helping you actually land a job.

The government pays people for not working, but does little to help them find or prepare for meaningful jobs.

So many societal structures are broken, just like the church, which all too often, doesn't look much like Jesus. I think this brokenness is a reasonable explanation for much of the global unrest we have been experiencing.

There is a pattern in each of these arenas:

- A societal structure is broken.
- People are being hurt by the unresponsiveness of their institutions.
- The powers that be hold change to a snail's pace to keep it from threatening their power and position.

48

- There is social unrest, because the institutions which are supposed to be serving us, are not.

I can think of three responses for dealing with these broken structures. The most intuitive one would be reformation. Try to fix what is broken. After all, these are time honored institutions and a little tweaking should fix things. As I previously indicated, this is a slow and painful route. You will be misrepresented and maligned. People have too much vested interest in the existing structure to take you seriously. In fact, you may not be able to do much at all.

Revolution is another option. However, revolts are about the past and present, rather than thinking ahead to the future. They also tend to be negative and bloody. Often the end game is something not much better than what was revolted against.

The third option is called criticizing by creating. It is not just complaining about the old systems, nor trying to change them. It is about making them irrelevant through new, creative approaches. It is experimenting and failing and trying again. It is risk-taking; defying conventional wisdom and discovering and doing what is truly in your heart, rather than fulfilling someone's expectations. It's about effectiveness; making sure something works. It's about values; honoring people over systems and self-interest.

Being coerced out of the church and pushed to the fringes made me an outsider and enabled me to see things more objectively. What I found was a church disconnected from its roots and its reality. The church bears little resemblance to its early days and even less to Jesus.

On the other hand, the church also seems to be disconnected from its cultural context and its market, i.e., all of those people who see it as irrelevant. I wonder what a pastor or denominational official would say about that? I have a strong feeling, based on a lot of experience that he might reply that the church is supposed to be separate from the culture as an example of being "set apart", which also means it doesn't change with every whim of society. Yet, if the church is disconnected from Jesus and the people it is supposed to love, it is in real trouble!

The prophets of old were all outsiders who railed against the establishment and dreamed of how things could be. The hope for the future is not with the core, it's with the fringe; the people pushed to the edges by our society. If the system is working fine for you, you won't see the need to change it. But, if you have been on the receiving end of injustice or disenfranchisement, it is a whole different story!

So, I have finally come to embrace my status as an outsider. I hope I am not self-righteous about it. I don't think it is the way for everyone. It is not a perfect path and I don't have everything figured out. Without a doubt, in many ways, I am the antithesis of my former self.

One time a few years ago, someone was seeking some pastoral advice as we were sitting at the kitchen table. My son piped up and said, "Pops is pretty much the same, only he ditched the suit, drinks beer, and listens to Metallica." That was his take. Honestly, I ditched the suit a good many years ago. I only dig a few Metallica songs, but in times past, I wouldn't have listened to them for a minute. I do, however, like a good cold beer, another former taboo for a good Baptist pastor.

The changes go considerably deeper than Nathan's humorous comment. I have changed, and I don't want to go back under any circumstances. I am not turned off by people who have different beliefs. I am not afraid to delve into those beliefs and discuss them. I don't feel that evangelism is all up to me. I believe more in a "go and show" approach than "a come and hear" one. I am less preoccupied by the past and the future and what people think of me. I am more alive in the moment. I spend a lot more time with my family. I listen to almost every kind of music known to man. I don't read many Christian books or listen to much Christian music, because I find God all over the place and in unlikely places. I love the shear spiritual depth I find in some secular music and writing, which surpasses much of the neurotic, self-improvement oriented Christian literature and syrupy Christian music. I don't align with either political party. I have learned that I love to write and stir up a little trouble now and then.

I sometimes wonder why God couldn't just leave me alone in my Christian and church leadership sub-cultural bubble. I wonder what actually has driven me on this quest. I tend to ask questions and be a little more open to change than a lot of people, but there was something deeper driving me. I was on a search for something real. I am looking for a faith that is real, a church that is real, and a life that is real.

For me, that is going to be something different than I started with. It is not a faith marked by mental ascent to axioms. It is not a church were faithfulness to Christ is equated to the faithful support of an organization. It is not a life in which matters of faith compete with the rest of life. It is a faith grounded in living, rather than believing, a church that serves everybody, rather than just itself, and a life in which faith is a natural part of each and every day.

Part 2

An Irreligious Jesus:

Surprised by his Humanity

Give up your good Christian life and follow Jesus.
– Garrison Keillor

Sadly, when I was a pastor, the significant differences between Jesus and the church were not a big deal to me. Sure, I could get excited preaching about Jesus' compassion or how he was counter-cultural. Yet, I somehow missed the fact that church was so different from Jesus. Or, maybe I excused the differences as necessary accommodations to the times or essential to have a sustainable business model. Still, these differences are so pronounced that people who have little association with the faith can easily see them and justifiably point a finger of blame at a church which doesn't look much like Jesus.

Christians are masters at losing their focus. The simple teachings of Jesus have been replaced by a compulsion to make God manageable through systematic theology, to make our life run smoothly (hence, all of the "how to" sermons), to have carefully crafted services that would convince guests we are "cool," to leverage our numbers into political power, and to build a large, successful organization.

All through those years of being in church, I learned a great deal about Jesus' birth, death and resurrection, and remarkably little about the years in between, i.e., his life. This pattern parallels the fact that I learned a lot about what I was supposed to believe and little about how to live in the real world.

In Bible College, my professors spiritualized some of the most valuable things about Jesus' life, robbing them of their purest, simplest meaning. They taught that everything he did, especially his healings and miracles, were signs to prove he was the Messiah and creator who had power over disease, demons, and nature.

I had the impression they did not want anyone to think Jesus did anything as a compassionate response to human need. That would sound too much like the "Social Gospel," a movement which focuses on improving conditions on earth. They felt the Social Gospel was too confined to the temporal and it looked like someone was trying to earn their salvation with their good works.

That, oddly enough, seemed to be the worst form of evil to these fundamentalists, who prided themselves on being concerned with the truly spiritual issues such as where one would be spending eternity, how to understand the Bible correctly, and how to live a life separate from the sinfulness of the world. Even though they thought of themselves as literalists, when Jesus did something that did not fit their theology, they found ways to explain it away.

But, Jesus is God, and, more than anyone or anything, he showed us what God is like. So, we should take the biblical accounts of Jesus' life at face value. Granted, they may also have prophetical significance, but it is foolish to overlook the meaning in his very actions.

Jesus often surprised people and almost always defied expectations. He made a lot of people mad and a lot of other people glad. After all, he had an authority problem and associated with outcasts.

five

Authority Problem?

Jesus had an authority problem. He took civil authority in stride, but railed against the religious aristocracy and intentionally broke imposed religious rules with great regularity.

The Political Authorities

The Evangelical church became a political force in the eighties. Jerry Falwell, Pat Robertson and James Dobson began articulating a "Christian position" on issues of national interest. Interestingly, it was always the same as the Republican position. They began with moral issues, moved on to "family values," and eventually had a position on almost every issue, including the military, international affairs, and taxes. They even supported specific candidates.

I am aware that Falwell is dead. As well, Robertson and Dobson are elderly and are no longer as much of a political force. Yet, all three were noteworthy power players just a few years ago. I remember how James Dobson was no friend of John McCain because he wasn't conservative enough and because he swore. In the 2012 election cycle, some evangelical leaders met in somebody's living room and chose Santorum as their man, but nobody cared. Fortunately, the influence of Evangelical leaders who tell us how to vote is waning.

Sincere Christians with sincere motives have become involved in politics because they have wanted to uphold Christian values on a national level. But, that's the problem. The United States is not a theocracy; it is a representative republic. Christians should be living out their values, rather than politicizing them and turning them into a national agenda. The influence of our daily lives will be far greater than any political power we may be able to gain.

A lot of Christians have a romantic view of our nation's past and its founding fathers. They believe our morals have gone to hell and that makes them both uncomfortable and mad. Far too much of our Christian political rhetoric has been an expression of that discomfort and anger. That's how we became famously perceived as homophobic, pro-life, and judgmental (and usually Republicans or Tea Party Activists). We are better known for what we are against than what we are for. So, popular opinion says we are self-centered, out of touch, angry, and uncaring. I only wish these perceptions were totally invalid.

How about replacing the negative campaign with love? How about loving gay people and speaking up to protect their rights because that's what you do when you love people?

I once interviewed an insightful and scholarly individual who said God's political agenda is love. He said this during a presidential campaign. Can you imagine how it would go over if a candidate said that his foreign policy was to love the people of all nations and ethnicities? Jesus loved all kinds of people, especially outcasts. There is our political agenda!

How about loving and helping the women who experience unplanned pregnancies, as well as the ones who have had abortions, and even those who provide the abortions? Again, it doesn't necessarily mean you're pro-abortion; it means you're serious about loving people the way Jesus did. That is where the real power lies!

This old system of Evangelical political power is almost dead, because people came to see that combining religious power with political power seldom, if ever, ends well. Power corrupts, and when a church leader who already has significant influence gains an audience or role as an advisor to someone with significant political power, it becomes difficult to remain a person of faith and character. Usually, the political agenda and the religious agenda are merged. Then, the politician sounds as though he shares the church leader's values, and the church leader is associated with platform positions that are not defensible from a Christian perspective. Before long, the gap between Jesus and the political/family values camp grows wider and wider, until they are incongruent. But, the alliances have already formed.

Let's be honest. Does it really matter to Jesus if the Ten Commandments are posted in a courtroom, if teachers can lead their students in a diluted, politically approved prayer, or if some people choose to say "Happy Holidays" rather than "Merry Christmas?" These things only matter to crusty old church members who remember when their perceived Christian ways were still in vogue. This type of indignation is born from the fact that the mores of culture have moved away from their comfort zone and the formerly popular Christian folkways. I just can't find any connection between these selfish issues of comfort and Jesus, who lived in a far, far worse political environment than twenty-first century America.

Jesus didn't seem to care about politics, other than to say we should pay our taxes.[1] His viewpoint seems strange when you realize his nation was occupied by a cruel militaristic superpower that had forged a partnership with religious leaders to form a corrupt theocracy. Israel and Rome had forged a government that was the ultimate blend of imperialism, militaristic might, religiosity, corruption, and cruelty. They crucified their enemies.

Followers of Jesus have every right and reason to be involved in government, because our system allows for our participation and it is only as strong as we make it. But, as Christians, we should judge ourselves rather than others, and endeavor to transform our image from hateful to loving, leveraging the real power of living life in the way of Jesus.

The Religious Authorities

In Jesus day, the Old Testament scriptures had been interpreted legalistically. Things were spelled out in detail in order to remove all of the guesswork about what it meant to obey (and what counted as sin).

According to the Talmud, the 6,200-page rabbinical commentary on the Old Testament, there are 613 mitzvot ("commandments") in the Torah. There are 248 positive mitzvot and 365 negative mitzvot given, supplemented by seven mitzvot legislated by the rabbis of antiquity.

This was the world of Jesus. Religious/political sects were self-appointed guardians of the law. Then, they commented even further on it, turning it into a straight-jacket that addressed ridiculous minutia, such as how far you could walk on the Sabbath without it counting as work and therefore violating the Sabbath.

Jesus accused them of making converts to themselves and not being a part of his kingdom. He called them whitewashed tombs, blind guides, and hypocrites. He hated the way they took advantage of people and put them into bondage. They were always trying to trap Jesus with their convoluted questions, but they always failed to outsmart him.[2]

He never seemed to miss an opportunity to butt heads with these people. You need to remember they were the most respected, and, supposedly, holiest people in the country.

Why did he dislike them so much? They misrepresented the faith, turning a relationship with God into an intricate list of ridiculous, impossible rules. They hurt people by misleading them and taking advantage of them financially, while regarding themselves as models of righteousness.

Today, some Christians still rant against liberals, gays, abortionists, and anyone who makes them feel a little uncomfortable. They complain about the U.S. becoming a secular country and abandoning its Christian heritage.

If Jesus walked the earth today, he would leave the president alone, but he probably would hammer some televangelists and others who are heavily vested into the religious structure that heaps guilt and duty on people in order to take advantage of them.

Money and power corrupt people. It doesn't matter if it's a city councilman, a pastor, or the President of the United States. Once people have a taste of power, they fight to hang onto it. Certainly, not every politician or religious official is corrupt, but their temptation is very real.

The church has done an impressive job of teaching that it and its leaders are sacrosanct and they always mean their church and the way they do church. However, there is nothing in Jesus' teaching or the New Testament to support this view. They usually take something from the Old Testament when Israel was a theocracy and try to apply it to the church to make their case. Some churches would not go as far as to outright teach that the church and its leaders are sacrosanct. Instead, they listen only to the views of likeminded leadership team members and disregard any divergent perspectives.

You have probably heard the expression, "Speak truth to power." It's the role of the prophet, the citizen, and the neighbor to keep powerful people accountable to those they are supposed to be serving. It's a worthwhile thing to do, especially in America, where citizen activism is a part of our foundation. It is also a worthwhile thing to do within the church. If we love the church, we will speak up when we see it misrepresenting Christ.

"Speaking truth to power" has its costs. It's a good way to be branded a troublemaker and someone who is angry at the church. Do it anyway! I don't mean become a chronic complainer, because anyone can do that. Instead, speak from a loving heart and be willing to be a part of the solution.

The Rules

If you were to read the Gospels without having any religious background, you would swear Jesus was doing everything he could think of to agitate the religious establishment of his day. He wasn't the ultimate hippie or a crazed rebel; he knew exactly what he was doing. He was defying man-made religious rules that made some people look bad and others look good, because God is loving toward all people, rather than regarding some above others. The dignity and worth of a human being is more important than any rule.

So, Jesus healed[3] people on the Sabbath, his disciples picked grain on the Sabbath[4], and he associated with all manner of outcasts including the worst of the worst.[5] These acts were serious religious violations with serious consequences.

Rules dividing people into separate groups should be broken. Rules ignoring human need should be broken. Any personal or societal barriers inhibiting us from being compassionate should be broken. Our piety needs to be swapped for a giant dose of humility. Our talk should be traded in for action. Our pride must be traded for a broken heart until we begin to value every individual. Instead of clean hands and a cold heart, we need to have dirty hands and a heart motivated by love, resulting in action, even when it makes us feel uncomfortable.

six

Loser-Lover

I like how Jesus loved such a broad cross-section of people, from the wealthy Zacchaeus to the blind beggar, but there is no question he had a soft spot for those who had been pushed to the far edges of society and were considered unacceptable. No wonder so many people still find him compelling today.

The Attraction

Why do we remember our wounds more than our encouragements? Maybe, it's because there are more of them. I don't know, but I do know they tend to become deeply etched in our souls. Maybe, it is because we walk a delicate balancing act in our psyche between feeling "I can" and feeling "I can't", and it takes just one person agreeing with either inner voice to convince us that voice is true.

I remember the middle-aged church member who said, "Why don't you go to college so you can amount to something?" It was after the second time I dropped out. I didn't care for her tone or the implications of what she said. In a rare moment of clarity when my thoughts and words came together, I said, "I probably will return, but I don't have to go to college to amount to something."

When I was going to college, I ran into the pastor of the messed-up Baptist church from my teenage years that I wrote about in the first part of the book. He had moved on to become a state denominational official. At the time, I was with my current pastor, who jokingly asked my former pastor, "You have a job for this guy down at the state office?" My former pastor replied, "Maybe something in janitorial." It was an intentional and hurtful dig, because he obviously didn't like me. He was such a jerk!

Recently an acquaintance referred to me as a "kept man" because I am not currently employed, at least not in the sense that I wake up in the morning and drive to my place of employment, put in eight hours and receive a paycheck twice a month. Fortunately, my wife does have conventional employment and that is how we have been able to stay afloat. Instead, I am developing my own business as an author, speaker, and consultant. It has been a long road for me to arrive at my present conclusion about employment, and it will probably be another long road until it becomes profitable. (So, thanks for buying this book!)

My point is, our friend had no idea how and why I left church ministry and what hell that was for me. She had no idea how I have looked daily for a job, or a better one, for years. She had no idea of all of the jobs I have had, even though each was a terrible match. She had no idea of the investment I have made in retraining myself. She had no idea how I had done volunteer work for years in hopes of eventually being employed in a community service position. She had no idea how much time I had put in to develop a home business. She had no idea of what I was currently working on. She had no idea that I stay as busy as people who are gainfully employed. She had no idea that, in all of my years leading up to this rough patch, I was unemployed for a grand total of one week. She had no idea about how agonizing all of this felt.

There are plenty of things people will do to make you feel like a loser, and there are, unfortunately, people who are born into being regarded as losers. There were enormous segments of the population who were considered losers in Jesus' day. Prostitutes, lepers, the disabled, people of other ethnic groups were all total outcasts. He was drawn to them; he focused on them.

I can't think of anyone in the gospels who had an encounter with Jesus and did not walk away from him encouraged; except for the powerful, the wealthy, and those who thought they were righteous.

If Jesus was walking around here today, we would find him by first finding the losers, the outcasts, and the marginalized.

"His personal outreach to people religion officially avoided was one of the most distinctive and shocking things about Jesus. Here, he was the Jewish Messiah who kept thumbing his nose at hundreds of years of Jewish tradition, religious authority, and unquestioned codes of behavior. He kept tearing down rules and traditions by saying hated Samaritans were okay, and despised tax collectors were loved by God.

"Whether it was befriending hookers, talking to Romans in public, or healing lepers without the express permission of the temple authorities, Jesus knew all about the kingdom of God including outsiders."[1]

Imagine a known drug addict, a gay couple, or a homeless person who needed some attention in the personal hygiene department walking into your church service. How would they be treated? Would heads turn? Why does something like this happen so rarely?

I am beginning to see that, with Jesus, there are no losers, just those who have trouble fitting in and those who society wants to ignore.

We need to find some "losers" and hang out with them to save our own souls.

The Parties

I cannot help but see the stark contrast between Jesus and present day Christianity. It is almost as if they are two completely different faiths; one separated, cloistered into its own subculture, the other on the streets, in the slums, and in the bars. One, trying to be holy through self-improvement and dissociation, the other being holy through relationships and involvement with people wherever they are, especially if they are shut out by the rest of the culture. One goes to church. The other goes to parties.

Jesus turned water into wine at a wedding feast. He went to a party at Mathew the tax collector's house, with a bunch of his tax-collector friends. At the time, tax collectors usually were dishonest, and often skimmed money off the top for themselves. It doesn't seem like Jesus ever turned down an invitation.

He was accused of being a drunkard, a glutton, and a friend of sinners. The last accusation was actually true and was never denied by Jesus.

Why would the Son of God go to parties?

"Jesus did not mechanically follow a list of 'Things I Gotta Do Today,' and I doubt he would have appreciated our modern emphasis on punctuality and precise scheduling. He attended wedding feasts that lasted for days. He let himself be distracted by any 'nobody' he came across...

In Bonhoeffer's fine phase, Jesus was 'the man for others'. He kept himself free – free for the other person. He would accept almost anybody's invitation to dinner; as a result, no public figure has a more diverse list of friends, ranging from rich people, Roman centurions, and Pharisees, to tax collectors, prostitutes, and leprosy victims. People liked being with Jesus: where he was, joy was."[2]

Where I live in the Great Lakes region, we have abundant outdoor festivals and concerts in our two warm months. Every outdoor event is in July or August, because the weather is just too iffy in the spring and fall. I love to be outside. I love music. I love people. And I love parties! So, we go to several of these events every year. Sometimes, when I look around and see people of all ages having a good time, I have had a strange, moving sort of feeling come over me. Actually, I have been moved to tears.

It certainly hit me at both my son and daughter's wedding receptions. There was something encouraging about seeing everyone have fun. People were eating and drinking, dancing and playing, joking and conversing, enjoying old relationships and making new ones. It's strangely healing. We need one another. We need to let our hair down and have fun. We need more parties!

Don't you think Jesus enjoyed mixing it up with people? Don't you think he enjoyed seeing people celebrate their marriage? He must have had fun watching the tax collector and Zealot (roughly the equivalent of an occupy activist and a corporate CEO) at the same party, along with some commercial fishermen known to be hotheads. I think he smiled and laughed with the best of them. He was probably an awesome dancer, too!

The "religious heat" hated that he went to parties. Everyone else loved it!

Go to more parties! Plan some of your own!

The Touch

Most of Jesus' miracles were healings. He healed all manner of people, all different ways, from simply speaking the words, to a touch of his robe, to forgiving sins, to applying mud to blind eyes. He noticed those who were ignored, the outcasts, the beggars, and those who were simply written off as having no hope. Today, don't you think we would find him with the HIV positive individual, the cancer victim, the homeless person, and the wounded and forsaken soldier?

Let's be honest, it can be depressing to hang out with these people; that is, until we meet the ones who, ironically, encourage us. I don't like being around people with disease or disfigurement. I hate feeling helpless to do anything for them. Yet, I'm not helpless. I can't miraculously heal them, but I can be their friend. I can help out with their incidental needs. I can listen to them. I can be a healer in that way.

Right now I have two neighbors with acute health issues. One moved to Florida for a double lung transplant. He just had the surgery, and he will have to stay in the area for two and half years. They had to figure out what to take with them in their move and what to leave here and they had to find a place to live in Florida. We are in touch through emails and texts. The other neighbor just had shoulder replacement surgery. There is surely some way I can be a healing, encouraging influence for these people!

I dream about being a powerful lover who is known for the way he makes time for people, gives them his undivided attention, asks them important questions, and is not afraid to put his arms around them and give them a hug. I would like to be the guy who leaves people feeling encouraged, loved, a little more healed, and with a smile on their face.

The Conversations

"The Gospels show Jesus quickly established intimacy with the people he met. Whether talking with a woman at a well, or a fisherman by the lake, he cut instantly to the heart of the matter, after a few brief lines of conversation these people revealed to Jesus their innermost secrets. People of his day tended to keep rabbis and "holy men" at a respectful distance, but Jesus drew out something else; a hunger so deep that people crowded around him just to touch his clothes."[3]

We get together with our friends Christie and Cory a few times a year, to try out new restaurants somewhere in or between Chicago and Milwaukee. (We live between Chicago and Milwaukee and they live in Milwaukee.) We eat. We laugh. We linger. That's what we do when we get together with them. They are "foodies." I am less discriminate and generally eat whatever is in front of me and am just thankful I didn't have to prepare it. They are especially adept at asking questions of the server and commenting about the food, which usually leads to a deeper conversation. They know how to draw people out.

I love people who are good at that; you know, those individuals who graciously draw strangers into a conversation and have a sincere interest in the life of somebody they just met. We all need connection with other human beings who enrich our lives. We love it when people are interested in us, but loving other people is, perhaps, even more rewarding.

Jesus ran the gamut with his personal conversations. He talked with a vast variety of people. The esteemed religious official, Nicodemus came to Jesus at night and had an in-depth spiritual conversation with him.

The Samaritan woman at the well in Sychar had a meandering conversation with Jesus, in which they talked about true satisfaction in life, the nature of worship, and her own difficult life. Jesus finally revealed his true identity to her and she was so excited she ran back to her village and left her water pot at the well.

He had an interesting encounter with a woman who had been caught in the act of adultery and was about to be stoned to death. He turned to the judgmental crowd who was poised to perform her execution and asked the person who was without sin to throw the first stone at her. One person walked away, then another, and another, until not one accuser was left. Jesus asked the poor woman, "Where are your accusers?" She replied there was no one left to condemn her. Then, Jesus said he didn't accuse her either and commanded her to go and sin no more.

I am doing better at this now, but I have always struggled to be free enough of my own preoccupations, agenda items, and insecurities to be fully present in the moment and spontaneously engage people. With his life, Jesus teaches us how to be fully engaged and fully engaging, totally present in the moment and totally interested in the other person.

The Stories

I wish I could spin a yarn like Garrison Keillor, but, alas, I am a concept guy, not a detail guy. Popular author, Donald Miller, recently tweeted, "A good story is more powerful than an army." Keillor has been spinning his meandering yarns about Lake Wobegon for nearly forty years, and Donald Miller has captured the hearts of a new generation of Christ-followers with his books, *Blue Like Jazz*, *A Million Miles in a Thousand Years*, and others. They are both extraordinary storytellers.

So was Jesus; he told about thirty-seven stories recorded in the Bible. He actually told many more, but these are the ones we call parables, or in today's terms we'd call them true myths.

I always loved The Parable of The Prodigal Son. When I was a preacher, I would put so much detail and pathos in it that my son would remind me it was only a story Jesus told to make a point (probably because he thought I was thinking about him).

Jesus could keep up with Garrison Keillor; actually, he could outdo Keillor, and yet all of his stories would be loaded with truth. Jesus talked about things people could relate to, like farming, wine, trees, sheep, baking, work, investing, marriage, and weddings. From the familiar, he would build a bridge to the unfamiliar truth he was teaching.

I mentioned earlier how I used to get mad when I would see someone getting the nods while I was preaching. Immediately, I called their spirituality into question. Then I would begin to talk louder. Christians can be boring, but I am convinced no one ever fell asleep when Jesus was talking because he was so real, so relevant, and so fascinating.

Recently, Erik Guzman, the producer and Vice President of Communications for the Key Life Network, hosted the syndicated radio program, *Steve Brown, Etc.* in Steve's absence. *Steve Brown, Etc.* is Key Life's way of living out and demonstrating God's grace. The guest list on the program is diverse, with people representing all sorts of takes on the Christian faith. Steve and Erik amuse me to no end, because you never know what they are going to say on the air. The program is as spontaneous, grace-filled, and edgy as one ever would dare to be on Christian radio. They deliberately push the envelope.

A few months ago, Erik hosted a program about sex. The guest contrasted the biblical perspective of sex being exclusively for marriage between a man and woman with modern day romance stories and pornography, as characterized by the movie *Magic Mike* and the bestselling novel, *Fifty Shades of Gray.*

Erik, and his co-hosts Zach and Kathy, did a superb job of asking insightful, honest questions. My buddy Erik also interjected a couple of laugh-out-loud parody commercials.

Because of this program, one station manager commented on their blog expressing his utter disgust. The station dropped the program. Unfortunately, this station manager reinforced all of the negative stereotypes about Christians; that they are out-of-touch, repressive prudes who care more about their own comfort than real people who struggle with real issues.

Jesus kept it real, relevant, and edgy. He also took a lot of heat for his teaching which was often shrouded in stories.

The Few

Jesus could and did draw a crowd, until his teaching became more cryptic; then people started scratching their heads and staying home the next day. It was as though he deliberately thinned the crowd, sending away the religious moths that always flew to the brightest light.

He selected a band of people to follow him and he was incredibly loyal to them. It was a crazy lot; a traitor, people with anger management issues, some of the guys from Deadliest Catch (commercial fisherman), a scumbag IRS agent (tax collector), and a person with ties to a terrorist organization that was trying to overthrow Roman rule (Zealot). Jesus would put them in new situations and afterwards he would ask them what they had learned. They were with him day and night. I would love to read their memoirs of their time with Jesus; all of the stuff not contained in the Gospels.

Almost everything meaningful in life happens in the context of relationships. Jesus' style of discipleship makes a strong case for mentoring, with small clusters of people and individuals coming together and learning from each other outside of the church walls and its orchestrated programs. It is quite a contrast to how we do church, with our massive Sunday morning presentations and well-planned programs.

"Jesus didn't dwell on ideas as much as he did the experience of real life. Don't mistake an essay describing rock climbing for actually strapping on a helmet and climbing seventy feet up the base of a cliff."[4]

We are only going to influence a few people in our lives. We ought to figure out who they are and what we want them to remember about us when we are gone. Try this: write your own eulogy and then try to live up to it. Think about the people who mean the most to you and what you want them to remember about you.

The Contrast

A few years ago, I was at a meeting with a bunch of community and church leaders who were facing a startling reality; a large church-based food pantry was closing down. At the meeting, there was also a presentation about how our community could move to more of a cooperative model, in which emergency food needs would be met and the entire community would benefit by having a much lower food bill. It would only require a small fee and a few hours of volunteering by its members. Those without the money for the fee could simply volunteer a little more. It was a brilliant and proven plan.

After much discussion, nothing happened, because the change would have been unsettling for the remaining churches running the food pantries. They could not conceive of another way of addressing the need. They found fulfillment in their involvement with the food pantries and did not want to see it threatened, even though they could have served in a similar way in the cooperative.

They just couldn't wrap their minds around the new concept and how it would make things better for even more people in the community. What they heard was someone wanted to shut down the food pantries and deprive them of the camaraderie and fulfillment they received from volunteering. The community leader who called the meeting quickly backed down from something that would have benefitted everyone.

During the course of the conversation following the excellent introduction to cooperatives, someone said something that rubbed me the wrong way. It came from the same guy who led the local Christian charity I had the job interview with that I wrote about in Part 1 of the book.

He related something he observed at his recent visit to a convenience store. He saw a young woman checking out ahead of him. She paid for her purchase using food stamps and her selections were completely non-nutritious. I don't remember the details, but you can imagine, maybe a Slurpee, a soda, some candy bars, or something like that. When she got into her car, it didn't immediately start; though it finally did.

Then, he shared what he thought at that moment. "Oh, I bet tomorrow she will show up or call us to help with her car repair, but I know she is wasting her money on Slurpees (or whatever it was)."

Even though he thought he was insightful and people nodded their heads in agreement, his tone was so condescending that I was agitated by his judgmental and arrogant attitude.

Maybe the young woman was operating out of ignorance, without the advantage of parents who taught her about managing finances, good nutrition, and personal responsibility. Maybe she didn't have the advantages many of us take for granted. Maybe she had a rough day and was self-medicating with junk food (I've done that way too many times.) Maybe she had a demanding boyfriend and was buying the stuff for him. We just don't know what her motivation was, but the guy telling the story felt as though she was intentionally abusing the system. Maybe she was, or maybe she wasn't, but the issue is his condescending response.

The fellow who told the story seemed to have let his heart grow hard and prideful; looking down upon the very people he was supposed to help.

I think Jesus' approach would be the polar opposite. My "friend" would have missed out on an opportunity to love someone and to help her; not just to meet an immediate need, but to have the chance to offer her friendship and maybe, even, help her to improve her situation in life.

So, I see a remarkable difference between that dude's hard heart and Jesus' tender heart, between his looking down on people who are less-advantaged and Jesus' seeking them out, between his arrogance and Jesus' humility.

I don't have vengeful thoughts toward this guy. He just provides me with some really good illustrations about what not to do. Seriously, I find negative experiences to be instructive. But, in all honesty, I have a long way to go, too, when it comes to seeing people like Jesus does and connecting with those who take me out of my comfort zone.

seven

Weird Agenda

Jesus was not only counterintuitive back in his day, even today there is still a gigantic contrast between his ways and the ways of the religion that goes by his name.

The Non-Agenda

- We have sacred creeds, sacred places of worship, sacred objects, and sacred leaders or clergy. Jesus had none of it.
- We are part of a subculture that insulates us from real life. Jesus talked about a different way of living real life.
- We obsess over trying to be better Christians. Jesus redeemed and restored us so we could reach our unique, individual potential to represent him and do his work here and now.
- We have Christian books, Christian music, Christian schools, and Christian t-shirts. Jesus didn't figure on using his name to create a brand.
- We focus on what happens when we die. Jesus taught us how to live.

- We have codified what it means to follow him and we have constructed a systematic theology to try to explain (and tame) God. Jesus just said, "Follow me."
- We have a church hierarchy of professionals and programs to make us better Christians. Jesus lived with his followers.
- We like to package things. So, we have a Sunday morning show with a carefully crafted sermon. Jesus taught standing in a boat and sitting on a hillside.
- We like to tell church members how to vote and we become upset when things don't go our way in politics. Jesus couldn't have cared less about the government.

The Likely Agenda

- Jesus probably would...
- Hang out with gay people.
- Reach out to those who have had an abortion.
- Take a liberal to lunch (a conservative, too). Maybe he would have lunch with both of them at the same time.
- Rip into some church leaders.
- Blow people's minds with his teaching.
- Have a "colorful" group of followers.
- Love hurting and broken people.
- Be strangely silent about politics, government, "the culture war", and "family values."
- Be the only person to bring Democrats and Republicans together.

If I were to attempt to make a complete list of the contrasts between Jesus and the church, it would never end. It is absolutely bizarre when you think about it. No wonder the church is messed up. No wonder its credibility is shot to hell. No wonder it has fallen on hard times.

Following Jesus in his day meant just that. That's how the cream of the crop, the young people with the most potential were educated. They followed their Rabbi for years. They lived and traveled together. The kids who were not the best and brightest learned a trade. But, Jesus broke with tradition and chose some pretty weird people to be his closest followers, to spread the Good News after his earthly ministry was complete.

There are no rules for following Jesus. You just stay with him, watch him; see what he does, how he responds; watch what he does when he is stressed.

He took his followers to the darnedest places. Think about where they wound up as they followed Jesus; you might find yourself in some of the same places. You might wind up...

- At parties with the most notorious people in town.
- At the graveside of a dear friend.
- In the public forum, (repeatedly) butting heads with powerful people who can put a contract on your life if they disagree with you.
- Watching Jesus play with children, when you want to be serious.
- Listening intently to what he says as people are preparing to stone to death a woman who was caught in the act of adultery.
- Overhearing him explain to a powerful and religious man how God has restored humans to their vaunted position
- Hanging out with whores who are attracted to him.
- Chatting with corrupt government officials and corporate fat cats.
- Panicking in the middle of nowhere, with thousands of admirers but no food.

- Listening to great stories.
- Watching the crowds thin and seeing some of them even turn against him.
- Breaking lots of stupid rules that misrepresent God and hurt people.
- Seeing amazing things that remind you why you're walking with God.
- Talking with all kinds of people from all walks of life about this very topic: "What does it mean to follow?"
- Running for your life as your leader is betrayed and tortured to death.
- Running to a cemetery to check out an unbelievable rumor.

These are just a few of the places where we will go when we walk with Jesus. We will be a thorn in the side of some powerful people and a friend to some powerless people, someone who is fully alive in the moment seeing God everywhere. We will be a lover of all kinds of people, who finds himself in all types of weird, new situations.

Oh, I forgot to mention, to be a faithful follower of Jesus you need to read your Bible more, pray more, stop looking at porn, never argue with your wife, have beautiful, completely compliant children, never miss Sunday services, tithe, take classes on how to be a better Christian, keep a beautiful lawn and home, and spend all of your free time in church activities.

(Or wait, maybe I didn't forget to mention it.)

I used to care more about that kind of religious stuff than about simply following Jesus, but that stuff always seemed separate from regular life. So, now I am trying to jettison religion and merge faith and life together to live a more integrated, true, whole life.

People have all different ways of following Jesus, but a lot of us are trying to find a stripped down, raw and real approach that makes more sense.

Following Jesus means doing the kinds of stuff he did, turning love into action.

Reminder to self: Watch, learn, reflect, mimic. Never let him out of my sight.

Jesus' way isn't complicated or convoluted. It's raw and real; interwoven with life rather than separated from it. It's not complex, but it is ultimately more challenging than anything religion or the church ever could dream up. The awesome part is that his way is real. It is about life. It is life. His way makes a difference. His way gives meaning to our lives.

Engage

I will close each of the three remaining sections with some ultra-practical ideas about interweaving these principles into our lives.

While I have experienced some movement in a positive direction for some of the following points of application, others are still rather aspirational for me. Honestly, one of the main reasons I included these application notes is to provide a practical focus for my own life. I hope you find it helpful too.

What does it mean for me to follow Jesus? If I think about it in daily-life, nitty-gritty terms, it looks something like this:

- I would stop worrying about the church and would not confuse it with Jesus or his kingdom. I would realize following Jesus is a personal matter and it is my responsibility to live in his ways as I go about my regular daily life. Community is vital, but how I follow Jesus is up to me.
- I wouldn't be afraid to "speak truth to power," whether the "power" is the church, the government, the corporate world, or politically correct ideologies. I also wouldn't be surprised if it makes some people pretty mad.
- I would make it a point to seek out those who need a little help or a little love and I would be their friend.

That takes an intentional daily focus as I become more aware of the people I meet in the normal course of life.

- I would become an all-out people-person who is highly interested in individuals and their stories. I would become a conversationalist, a great listener, a good asker of questions, and I would be honest about my own failures.
- I would become a big-time partier, attending and hosting lots of parties and gatherings. I would know how to have a good time and how to help people have a good time (without getting drunk).
- I would be a "hugger" and be more sensitive to people's real needs. I would take risks to do something to help people.
- I would help make their day a little brighter and I would be with them in their darkest times.
- I would become a better storyteller because of the sheer power of a meaningful story.
- I would invest heavily in the most important people in my life.
- I would look for chances to surprise people with grace.
- I would look for new opportunities to connect with people who take me outside of my comfort zone.
- I would believe Jesus is who he said he was and I would not try to earn his favor but would bask in his love and grace.
- I would devote my life to learning to love people like he did.

Part 3

An Irreligious Church:

Shifted into Reality

The church desperately needs creative heretics. A 'creative heretic,' an independent thinker, is an example of the 'unbalanced' force to which Newton refers in his first law of motion. Only the person who breaks with tradition can change the direction of an institution. A heretic is not an enemy of God but one who is more interested in truth than in tradition.
- John Sloat, A Handbook for Heretics

I keep running across people who are pessimistic about the current state of the church, but still manage to be optimistic about its future. Randy McRoberts is one of these optimistic pessimists. He explains why in his blog post entitled, "Demise and Rebirth."

"The evangelical church as we know it will not survive much longer.

The church will, of course, survive. The gates of hell will not prevail against it.

But the evangelical church-growth megachurch seeker-sensitive monstrosity we have built is as good as dead already.

People are on to the scam. We promised them Jesus and we gave them a social club, a program of entertainment, and an obligation to pay for those things and the buildings that house them and the people who dream them up. People are bailing. The vision casters have been nearsighted. The temple of Dagon is falling around us.

Already in our area we are seeing strong traditional evangelical churches in financial trouble. When smart people see financial trouble on the horizon, they get out before they have to own the financial trouble.

When a church is all about money, money will be its death.

Denominational structures will go first. They are already shredding themselves.

And by the time I'm ready to die, all those buildings of mega-church wannabes will house flea markets.

What will the church look like in the future? Nothing like what you probably think of as church; that is certain.

Your church will be more like what you think of as a small group today.

Leadership structures will be flexible and dynamic.

Your church won't own property.

No one in your church will be paid by the church.

Your church will demonstrate love for one another like you've never seen before.

Your church will be like your family instead of like your club.

You will be both a disciple and a mentor.

I say, bring it on."[1]

The institutional church is in big trouble, due to loss of membership, decreasing income, sexual scandals, and a judgmental persona. It is perceived as anti-gay, compassion-challenged, unlike Jesus, and generally irrelevant. Will it gradually evolve into the kind of church Randy longs for?

To varying degrees, the church can and will change. The changes will probably be slow and the church will hold on to as many bags from the old days as it can, for as long as it possibly can, but it still has the potential to be a powerful force for God and for good in the world. Actually, there are a few remarkably positive examples of local churches already having made fantastic shifts, giving them a vital witness for Christ in their community.

eight

A New Framework

I love the church. What's not to love about a community representing Christ to the world? It's a beautiful ideal, even though the reality is, all too often, a different picture. There is a significant potential in thousands of churches across our land. In this section, I will discuss some shifts that can help a conventional church move into the present reality. When we see these changes begin, people like me will give the institution another look.

From Criticizing to Creating

This is actually a shift for those looking back over their shoulder at a church they left behind or the one they never embraced. Think of it as something of a disclaimer, defining the type of scrutiny I believe the church should receive.

There must be workable suggestions along with the catalog of problems. There must be energy going into creativity and not just criticism.

Should we criticize the church? Only if we love it! If I didn't love the church, I wouldn't care about it enough to criticize it, or else, I would criticize it in a mean-spirited and destructive manner. If, however, someone you love is involved in something that is misrepresenting her and is ultimately destructive, you won't just let her continue to walk toward the cliff until she falls off. You will say something!

We all have faults and blind spots, so lobbing criticism at anyone or anything is pretty easy. Lord knows, anyone who is acquainted with me easily could make a long list of what they think is wrong with me and no doubt many of the items would be quite true.

So, listing faults is sort of like shooting ducks in a barrel. When you shoot ducks in a barrel, you will probably wind up with a few dead or wounded ducks, or at least, a few really, really mad ducks.

I don't want to wound anyone in the church and I don't want to make church-goers and church leaders mad, but the latter part is out of my control. My intent is to show the church some possible ways forward, because my crazy story gives me both the perspective of an informed practitioner and that of a seasoned outsider.

It takes much more thought to be on the solution side of things than it does to point out what's wrong. Yet, the problem needs to be identified in order to suggest ways to improve. Some people don't like it when we talk about the church's problems, but identifying the problem is always the first part of making things better. However, that is only the beginning point. Then, the hard work of problem solving and improvement must begin.

Many of us have almost given up on this type of reformation, but some wonderful things could happen if the church was open to honest evaluation and change.

From Piety to Honesty

Earlier, when I was recounting my church experiences, I didn't tell you about one couple with whom we shared life. Their kids were the same ages as ours and went to school together. Actually, this was true of two different families through the years. I didn't tell about the kind couple who shared their boat with us. Whenever we wanted to, we could just go to the lake, punch in the dock security code, get the key, and take off in their speed boat.

A couple of older families sort of adopted us, helping us out financially, even though the church paid me a fair salary. One guy helped me build a large deck on the back of our home. Another put several hundred-dollar bills in my hand to help me buy the materials.

We are still close friends with one family, even though it's been twenty years since I was their pastor. We live a few hundred miles apart, but we still get together occasionally and pick up right where we left off. I officiated at one of their son's weddings and, unfortunately, at another son's funeral. Their daughter used to babysit our kids and later was a caregiver for Patty's mother. We know each other's parents, children, and grandchildren. Our families are intertwined and I am so close with the mom that we kind of think of each other as siblings.

I didn't tell you about my friend who was the most dedicated administrative assistant I can ever imagine. We developed and shared a powerful vision together. We endured abuse and commiserated together, too.

I didn't tell you about the young leadership team that helped me totally re-envision and re-build a church. We didn't just do church; we did life together. We were family!

My conclusion is that church-going people are just like everyone else, both kind and cruel, loving and self-righteous. They are just people, but we tend to expect more of them because they wear the tag "Christian."

If becoming a Christian is just ascribing to certain mental axioms, how could we possibly expect more of Christian people? But, if loving Jesus is about a new way of living, not just something to believe, and not just a club to join, then maybe the bar should be a little higher.

We all screw up, royally at times, and we need to be honest about it. At the risk of sounding crass, I must say some Christians act like their shit doesn't stink. But, when we are mean to others, disenfranchise them, or when we are prideful or exclusive, then our shit out-stinks everyone else's because we are misrepresenting the very one whose name we carry with us. The church has enough to judge within their own parameters without pointing their finger at those outside.

If we could move from piety to honesty and from pretension to safety, we would be healthier and more gracious individuals. We have to find a way to live somewhere between arrogance and guilt in a place of freedom and grace. Until we experience it, we will never grant it to others.

From Ignoring to Shifting

My first car was a 1966 Mustang with a standard transmission and a floor shifter. I loved to listen to that sporty little car roar as I ran it through the gears to impress my friends. I loved that awesome surge of power.

If you play guitar, you hear chord changes without anyone telling you to play a different chord. In the same way, when your drive a car with a standard transmission, you can hear when it's time to shift gears. When those RPM's get up to a certain level, you hear that whine of the engine and transmission letting you know it time to shift to the next gear.

The church has wrung every last bit of usefulness out of many of its methodologies and folkways. Like a car in first gear, the church is loud, calling attention to itself, grinding it out, trying to power through the resistance of culture. As the whine reaches a higher and higher pitch, it quickly enters the danger zone for the transmission and engine. The church is in the danger zone as evidenced by decreasing attendance, an aging constituency, shrinking revenues, diminished influence, and whole generations who feel disenfranchised. Spiritually inclined people are leaving. Others are never even darkening the church's doorway, as they seek different ways to express their faith. Droves of people consider church to be totally irrelevant.

If you think the church has made a lot of changes in recent years, you're right, but these changes have been simple tweaks when an extreme makeover is needed. We have replaced the piano and organ with rock bands. We traded the expository sermon for the topical, practical, application-oriented talk about marriage, finances, and other issues in life. We have satellite churches, electronic fund transfers for online donations, downloadable sermons, and massive projection and sound systems.

Inside the church, we think of these tweaks as great advances, but the perspective of those looking from the outside in is quite different. As a matter of fact, twenty-five percent of outsiders believe the church has become worse.[1]

These people think the church has run off the rails; that our current expressions of Christianity seem disconnected from Jesus and what the church ought to be.

That helps explain the mass exodus from church.

People are avoiding the church, turning away from it in droves.

"Fifty-one percent left the religion of their youth because their spiritual needs were not being met. Today there are 31 percent fewer young people who are regular churchgoers than in the heat of the cultural revolution of the 1970's."[2]

I find it interesting that this decline in church attendance is happening when people are so spiritually inquisitive, searching for some sense of transcendent meaning. The church no longer has a corner on the market for spiritual expression.

By 2025, George Barna projects only one-third of the population will rely on a congregation as the primary means for expressing their faith. The other two-thirds will express their faith through other types of faith-based communities or the arts.[3]

My message to church leaders is, "Wake up!" Think about the people who feel disenfranchised by what is supposed to be a grace-oriented community! There is something more valuable than keeping the sheep that are already in the fold happy, re-teaching the people who should already know better, following the latest megachurch trend, and protecting your own job. How about re-aligning the church with its roots and with Jesus, in a way that connects with people in your place and time. It's time to shift gears!

nine

Right Side Up

The original vision of an organization becomes dimmer and dimmer as time goes on. Eventually, it will fall into maintenance mode. That's when the focus turns from outward to inward, and from service-oriented to protectionist. There are some specific shifts the church needs to make to obtain relevance.

From Top Down to Bottom Up

Why are people serving organizations or institutions whose real purpose is to serve them? The government, organized to protect our freedom, takes larger and larger chunks of our freedom and our income to feed its ever-increasing appetite. The corporation sells us products that need further instruction and repair, but fails to provide decent service. Social service agencies dole out money and programs like they were McDonald's, but have to keep their clients dependent upon their services so their funding will continue. Churches that are supposed to help us live in the way of Jesus and fulfill our place in his kingdom, instead train us to dutifully support an ever-teaching, seldom-doing, insider-focused, money-sucking organization. It is the great bait-and-switch and people are on to it!

When I was a pastor, I put considerable stock in my leadership team. I knew, appointed and trusted each person. The rest of my fledgling church consisted mostly of down-and-outers or individuals who seemed less-than-dedicated to the church. When they countered an idea the leadership team came up with, we would say, "They just don't get it."

Maybe, we didn't get them! Maybe, there were two visions for the church; the one that reflected where we were trying to take the church and the other where it actually was.

We have made the church into an organization you join. Members have certain privileges and responsibilities, but the authority lies with the church. Once you join, you hear about the expectations: "Here is what we believe and you need to agree with it. Here are our financial needs and you need to sacrificially and faithfully support them. Here are our programs and you need to get 'plugged in'. Here are our leaders and staff, you need to listen to them and respect them. Here is our path to discipleship; you need to take these classes."

This mindset developed from our passion to build a strong church and our desire to make our expectations clear. But, it has become a problem because we have equated being a faithful follower of Christ with being a loyal church member! We have confused supporting an organization with a way of living. We have formulated a narrow and organizational view of what it means to be a follower of Jesus. Unfortunately, the seat of power for this model of expressing our faith lies clearly with the organizational mechanism, rather than in relationships, life itself, or even in Jesus.

The church always looks like its culture, even if it is several years behind. The Roman Catholic Church looked like the prevalent system of the day, the Roman Empire, with its hierarchical, authoritarian structure. Modern American churches resemble the prevalent structure of our day, the corporate business world, with their CEO-ish senior pastors, staff, mission statements, and defined processes.

When examining what the Bible says about pastors, elders, and deacons, it's hard to tell what is descriptive and what is prescriptive. Is it a blueprint for how the church should be organized for all time and in all cultures? Scholars have been debating the details of church leadership and organization for as long as there has been a church.

We can say, for sure, that top-down church leadership is a turn-off for most people. It feeds the pride of the leaders and ignores God's working in each individual, while assuming everyone needs the same approach or must choose between the same predetermined options.

People don't trust organizations to have their best interests at heart and for good reasons. Organizational proponents want to build their organization so it has greater power, wealth, and influence; whether it is Wal-Mart or your local First Baptist Church. So, they try to encourage people to support it, contribute to it, and staff it.

People don't trust leaders anymore. That bubble has been burst too many times in the corporate world, government, and the church.

However, God is at work in each individual in unique ways. It is up to church leaders to inquire about those unique ways and partner with the work He is already doing in their lives.

How about serving people, instead of treating them like cattle to herd through our discipleship process in order to build up our organization? What if we honored God and honored them by working with them for the sake of Christ's kingdom and not our own?

What if our community, our circumstances and our people determined the nature of the church's ministry, rather than the church dictating it from the top down? It would be slow, messy, labor intensive, and would require an army of prepared people to facilitate. But, at least it would be real, and full of potential. It would be an improvement over trying to herd people through programs and encouraging them to serve the organization.

Here is an idea that just might work. Suppose the pastor takes his charge of preparing people for the work of the ministry seriously and develops a group of well-trained mentors/life coaches/spiritual directors (whatever you chose to call them). The training for these individuals would be extensive, and the bar would be set high. Everyone coming into the church would be made aware of this mentoring/life coach service so they can take advantage of it if they want.

The mentor would meet with the new person to hear their story and to help uncover some steps to assist the person in moving forward. This might involve emotional healing or opportunities to prepare for some type of ministry. The mentor would also be in the person's life for the crises, celebrations, and teachable moments that come along. He would have someone with whom he can discuss how things are going. The pastor would become the facilitator and coordinator of the mentors, not the guy who does everything. Then, whole new waves of something real and meaningful would begin happening in people's lives!

If this sounds too much like another church program that makes you feel like a tiny cog in a giant church machine, vulnerable to abuse from those in positions of authority, then I need to take a moment to explain the differences. The mentors would need to be carefully screened, as well as trained not to impose their desires upon the people they help. Their role is to come along side of the person, to help them fulfill their God-given potential. So, it would need constant, high-level monitoring.

From Professional to Volunteer

This shift is closely related to the previous one. When I was a pastor, there was a tendency among pastors to gauge a church's success by the attendance, the size of their building, and the number of staff members. I know; it sounds rather worldly, but it is true. We believed that the more staff we can hire, the more will get done, and the more the church will grow. That presupposes the idea of building an organization, rather than serving the people in the community and figuring out how to give away the gifts your church possesses.

Are professionally trained, paid clergy truly producing what we hoped for in the church? I have a lot of questions about the training professional clergy people receive because it focuses on becoming an expert in biblical languages and theology, rather than focusing on real life stuff. I also have a lot of questions about the ridiculously wide array of expectations congregants place on pastors. He can't possibly be an inspirational preacher, a gifted musician, a warm people person, a hospital and hospice chaplain, a corporate quality CEO, a dynamo, a gentle soul, a man of God, and have a perfect family. No wonder so many pastors turn to porn or somehow crash and burn!

Congregants want a hire a professional to do it all for them, rather than doing what they should be doing themselves. The congregation leans on the pastor for their spiritual nurture, to be the person who shows up in times of crises, and for initiating all things ministry related. We need to assume responsibility for ourselves and for those in our world, rather than outsourcing it!

Megachurches have responded by hiring a pastor for every area of ministry...worship, youth, children, small groups, administration, etc.

What if we moved away from the idea of building an organization and instead tried to give away everything we can? We could begin by giving away the ministry to volunteers. Then, their gifts will be expressed, more ministry will happen, and the church will have more money to use for other outwardly-focused ministries.

The role of pastors would shift more to one of a facilitator and coordinator of ministry. Pastoral education could focus more on working cooperatively in the community and building coalitions. He could learn how to map community needs and assets to help his constituents through community-based development.

The church's function is to equip people to live like Jesus in the real world, preparing and encouraging them to fulfill their unique role in Christ's kingdom.

The emphasis, then, would move from knowledge to action, from proclamation to living out the gospel, from inviting people to come to going to them, from building an organization to serving the community, from leading to facilitating, from hoarding to giving away.

From Programs to Relationships

It has been forty years since I was in high school. I probably would flunk a content-oriented test for any of my courses, because I just don't remember that stuff. But, I do remember two teachers. Mr. Blakely was a very intelligent social sciences teacher who taught our International Relations Class. I remember how he shut up a rowdy classroom as I was ready to give a report. Somehow he showed he believed in me and he sparked my interest in knowing what was going on in the world.

I also remember Mr. Wells. We called him Dr. Wells because he seemed like a mad scientist to the students in our Advanced

Biology class. We took some remarkable field trips; finding wounded geese in a wildlife refuge and videoing untreated sewage as it ran into the Missouri River. He was so passionate about his field of study that he created a new awareness in me.

Gathering people together and lining them up in rows, so they can look at the back of each other's heads and listen to a professional inspire and correct them is not usually the most effective way to help people move forward toward their potential in Christ. Neither is herding them up in classrooms and running them through pre-packaged program created by another megachurch.

Trying to teach people into Christlikeness is not only ineffective; it can be dangerous. The scripture itself says "knowledge puffs up, while love builds up."[1] I have seen too many extremely knowledgeable, arrogant people who just wanted more biblical knowledge and more reassurance that they were among the elite few who understood the Bible correctly. We don't need more knowledge, but rather more loving and living like Jesus.

Jesus had a remarkably different approach. His followers lived and traveled with him. He occasionally sent them off on a mission they felt unprepared for, and then asked them what they learned when they returned. They went where he went and encountered what he encountered. They lived with Jesus, did his work, and then talked about it.

Preaching holds some potential for inspiring us to begin a course of action, but its effectiveness has been vastly overrated. It might give us a little information and inspire us to further consider something, but it doesn't usually help us get out of the huddle and put the play into action.

Classes can expose us to new bits of knowledge, but we usually already know what we are supposed to be doing or not doing. There is a difference between living life in the way of Jesus and learning algebra and they require different approaches.

Where does life make up its mind? How personal change happens is a bit of a mystery, but I can tell what has impressed me down through the years. It has nothing to do with content, and everything to do with people and how much they cared.

Any way of doing church will be successful if the people love one another, welcome new people with that same love, and help them fulfill their God-given dreams and potential. If you love people and give them an opportunity to do what they love, they will love you back! How do you program that? You don't! You model it! You let it build, little by little until it becomes a pervasive force.

It is sadly funny how we have made our faith all about mere statements of belief and determining who is "in" and who is "out," rather than actually living and loving like Jesus.

Love happens in relationships. From a leadership perspective, maybe the most crucial thing we can do is to have real relationships ourselves, complete with all their risks and potential hazards. We can also encourage relationships by making space for them to happen. Social and ministry events can help provide that space, but not loading up the church schedule is probably the single most important thing we can do. That way, people can naturally develop relationships in their neighborhoods and wherever they normally find themselves.

Programs are a cerebral approach to a relational need. They are the quick fix that usually doesn't fix anything. They are the easy way out. They may have some effectiveness, but nothing beats what happens when people love each other.

From an Organization to a Group of Friends

My best church experience was when the church I pastored went through a rebirth. Our small groups became like individual churches where the participants experienced true community. All kinds of needs were spontaneously met. No programs were needed. People were given rides to the doctor's office. Individuals helped others pay their utility bills. Furniture was donated. We cared deeply for one another, even though we always didn't have a lot in common with each other. These groups were a place where people could be honest and they were a place where people honestly cared for each other.

Is there any more normal and natural way to follow Jesus than a group of friends getting together and talking about it? Because they are friends, they don't just gather around programs, they are already in each other's world. What if they genuinely love each other and want other people to experience the same kind of love? Isn't that the church?

What if the church became just that; friends getting together to talk about how to follow Jesus and to learn to love those around them? I can hear some program-oriented church person, asking, "Well, what about...and what about...and what about..."

The church is not an organization! It is hard for me to imagine that Christ intended to begin an organization. He redeemed and restored humanity, beginning a new way of living, loving him, and joining with him in his kingdom.

Almost every time I discuss the church, people immediately think about the organization. It is not an organization; it is an idea! In our world, the idea was expressed by an organization and throughout history the organization did some remarkably good things and some horribly wrong things, all in the name of Christ.

It makes no sense to imply that to be the church, we must have a building, staff, or programs. These were put in to place to carry out the idea, but we became overly dependent upon them, and we confused the methodology with the idea and the whole mess became an institution.

The church is a community that reaches out to demonstrate who Christ is. It is not a club of intellectual clones or a hive mind.

We have tried to control people's minds by saying, "This is what you must believe for it to be the real deal. Otherwise, we won't let you in." We have tried to control their actions by saying. "This is how to show you are a good Christian; you attend, you participate, and you give."

That is the way we work, not how God works! It just sounds wrong when we say you have to believe just like us before we will fully accept you into our community and now that you are in the community, you need to do this stuff to keep our organization going.

It sounds like Stepford Christians! The 1975 film, *The Stepford Wives*, (starring Katharine Ross) and the 2004 remake (starring Nicole Kidman) was set in the fictional town of Stepford, Connecticut. In Stepford, all the wives were all impossibly beautiful, submissive, zombie-like beings. It turned out they were actually robots!

Our emphasis on intellectual agreement with various statements of doctrine is not transformative. Seeing the love of God in action is. Being around followers of Christ and participating with them in following the way of Jesus opens our hearts and minds to believing what he said and what is said about him in the scriptures.

I know some churches have taken a stab at becoming more relational, usually less than successfully. You have to be careful, because nothing feels weirder than being lumped together with people who don't care deeply for one another.

Perhaps, the key is simply to encourage community and facilitate it. If some friends want to get together to do this kind of stripped-down church, leadership could provide some basic training and support for the facilitator. You would have to be careful to let it take its own course and not suffocate it with expectations. Most churches are too fearful that some people might have an original thought that does not align with the church teaching and structure to allow a group that type of independence.

Then there would be less emphasis placed on the large group gathering. Certainly, all the time and preparation that goes into it has gotten out of hand. Maybe, the large group would meet less frequently, like monthly.

This is a less organizational and more natural way of being the church. It sounds like a refreshing breath of fresh air to me.

From Gathered to Scattered

It must have been nearly ten years ago when Aaron, the Student Community Pastor at the church I was attending, sat in my car in front of the church building. We had just finished going out for lunch and were having our usual conversation about the sins of the church. Specifically, we were discussing the hope this new thing called "The Emerging Church" was stirring up. Our conversation continued as we drove back to church. I remember his words vividly, "One thing I don't understand is why we have to come to this building for everything." A lot of people don't get that, especially younger people.

"When Christianity was born, it was the only religion on the planet that had no sacred objects, no sacred persons, and no sacred places. The Christian faith was born in homes, out in courtyards, and along roadsides."[2]

"In the United States alone, real estate owned by institutional churches today is worth over $230 billion. Church building debt, service, and maintenance consumes about 18% of the $50 to $60 billion tithes to churches annually."[3]

There is nothing like a massive church "campus," built on several acres of prime real estate that looks like a shopping mall, to save the world.

Why do you have to travel to a building for activities centered on faith and ministry? Is that building sacred space, or is every place sacred space? Is God somehow geographically confined? Do we go there just because it is a pleasant place for people to gather, or because we need to justify the enormous mortgage? Why is everything so centralized?

I can think of three reasons. It allows for control, it allows professionals to lead, and it gives us a cozy, sequestered place to practice our rituals. Quality control is an issue with most churches. If you have little groups meeting all over the place, how will you control what is going on?

It would be a significant step toward integrating faith into real life if we took it out of the special building and put it into homes, coffee shops, and bars; wherever life normally happens.

Like so many things I have suggested in this section, it is a matter of training people and then releasing control. Then, there would be a much greater chance of experiencing real community, having more real discussions, and a sense of belonging in a more intimate, normal setting.

From Sanctuary to Community Center

At one point, during a community festival-of-kindness event, I walked to the upper bleachers of the community center and looked down on all that was taking place. Hundreds of families were receiving free groceries, free health screenings, and a whole array of agencies along with hundreds of volunteers were on hand to help people. While this annual event-oriented approach has its limitations; it was encouraging to see ten churches and five hundred volunteers working together to serve the people of their community. When I sat down to chat with people who were waiting to receive groceries, I would make small talk and then say something like, "We are just trying to show a little of Jesus' love today. I hope it helps out."

What if we lived out the Gospel every day, instead of saving it for an annual event?

How many times have you seen an old, abandoned church building in a not-so-great area of town; its congregation either diminished or moved to the burbs? Just when the neighborhood most needed a kingdom presence, it has been left high and dry.

How often have you driven by a beautiful church building on a weekday and seen it surrounded by a totally vacant parking lot?

What's wrong with this picture? Expensive real estate is being used exclusively for insider purposes and only a few hours a week, at that. People in the poorer areas of town have helplessly watched as all of their resources have moved away, including their churches, allowing for the further deterioration of the neighborhood on so many levels.

There is a basic problem with the church's outreach approach of "come and hear." It doesn't work! It doesn't mean anything! It doesn't cost us anything! It says, "Come to our place. Dress like us. Listen to our guy. Be like us, and then, maybe, eventually, when you make a profession of faith and go to some classes, we will accept you." It reduces the life and message of Christ to a little show and something cerebral to sign off on.

What if the church, once again, became the center of the community? What if our building became the community center? What if we looked for tangible ways to live out the love of Christ and to be the Gospel? What if the church collaborated with other community organizations and housed their services and offices, benefitting the agency, the church, and the people who live in the area? What if the senior pastor became more of a coordinator? What if the local church building was a heavily used facility that was almost constantly occupied? What would that do to the witness of the church in the community?

If that happened, there would be a beautiful renewal of old and underutilized church buildings, congregations, neighborhoods, and lives. What's stopping us? We will have to give up some control, stop worrying about the building showing signs of use, work together with other organizations, and get real about the Gospel!

From Build to Give Away

Almost all of the conferences I went to as a pastor were about building the church, increasing attendance, offerings, and participation in ministries. We were wrong!

This is the overarching principle for all the shifts I have mentioned so far. It strikes at the basic purpose of the church. The Church represents Christ on earth through its community and desire for others to come to faith and to follow Christ.

So, how do you do that? We built a self-serving organization that became the antithesis of our mandate!

Because we have built this organization, now we have to keep it going. Our mission to focus on others switched to everything being about us, the insiders. You have to keep the sheep happy, or they will stray. You have to teach them, even though they should be assuming responsibility for their own spiritual formation. You have to coddle them, or they won't feel loved and will leave. You have to inspire them, entertain them, teach their children, and provide a full slate of services, or they will go somewhere else. We have to build nicer buildings, hire more staff, and raise the finances to support all of this.

What if we built the church around giving away everything we could? What if we gave away the ministry to volunteers? What if we gave away our building to be used as a community center? What if we gave away our expectations for our senior pastor to hold our hand, and instead, let him train people who have a vision of their own? What if we let him coordinate and facilitate this ministry of loving others in meaningful ways? What if we abandoned our desire to be served through an array of church ministries and instead joined in being a part of the great giveaway? What if our strategic mission was to figure out to love the people around us in real, tangible ways; to actually show them Jesus?

From Trendy to Local

At one of the churches we attended, the pastoral staff frequently went to conferences. This resulted in a church that flowed on the tides of the latest trends espoused by the megachurches and their gurus. This church was forever tweaking their mission statement, ministry names, and structures. At the newcomers' lunches, they talked about how they were different and I almost choked on my sandwich as I began listing in my mind the churches I knew that were near clones. They all went to the same conferences and read the same books. They all had the same rockin' church band, the same practical teachings, the same titles for various staff members, and the same discipleship pathway.

To make matters worse, megachurches started birthing satellite churches which are exact clones of the mother church. Some of them even video-cast the sermon from the main church.

Churches are not factories, and we are not producing a product, we're dealing with people! Every community is not the same!

All of this indicates that there has been remarkably little reflection about what each local church should be like as they consider their people, their time, their place, and their opportunities.

What if, before any pastor was allowed to go to a conference, he first had to talk and pray with people in his own community, to find out what was going on and what they needed? What if he had to work with a team to develop an approach that was right for his unique community?

People have become so tired of cookie-cutter churches, they don't even check out a new church in town because they believe it will be just like the rest. These churches are usually copied from the same megachurch model. Many of them are unashamedly franchised copies of a local "mother church." Just like you know what to expect when you go to a McDonald's, wherever it is, the same is true for these franchised churches.

But, when church leaders start praying and talking with people, they have the opportunity to do something that will have outsiders taking notice about what an incredible contribution the church is making to community life.

From Performance to Reality

When I was a pastor, the Sunday morning service was "the thing"! We brainstormed, planned, practiced, studied, rehearsed, and critiqued, trying to get it just right. It consumed enormous blocks of time every week. We wanted to create an impression and illicit a specific response. It was theater.

I enjoyed parts of that approach. The challenge of creative communication and using the arts was a lot of fun, but it was still premeditated theater.

People don't live in an imaginary land. They live in reality.

A happy song, followed by a deeper one, followed by a meditative one, followed by a celebratory one is not going to change most people's lives. A dramatic sketch that sets up the topic, followed by a sermon that delves in a bit deeper, ending with the opportunity for a "life changing" commitment probably isn't going to do much either.

A beautiful auditorium full of beautiful people, all of whom who are "fine," is, frankly, a little creepy. What if we are not "fine"? And who, by the way, is "fine" every Sunday?

My chief grievance with the church is that it just isn't real. Therefore, it is not meaningful or effective. After a while, participation becomes either an addiction to our little emotional high experience, a social event to see our friends, a responsibility to our little church job, or an exercise in sheer duty.

That's why mentoring relationships and small group discussions have a greater potential for being meaningful. We feel freer to be ourselves in those types of settings.

Large group services have their limitations, but if they were a little more real it would be a huge improvement. There has to be freedom to be honest from the platform, but not in a voyeuristic way, where people try to out-shock each other. People simply need to be given permission and encouragement to be honest. It means people other than the pastors need to be allowed to speak and to tell their story. It means every Sunday service does not follow the same pattern. It means there are avenues for people who want to take a next step. It means walking away from the church building feeling like someone else understands and you are not all alone.

Honesty heals and it celebrates grace. When we are honest, God does awesome things.

ten

Stop Believing, Start Living

The previous shifts were all related to the methodologies of the church; the next few are more theologically-oriented. When I first began to experience a disconnect with church as I had known it, my complaints were about methods. When I began to read the thoughts of others, I realized that I had some problems with the prevalent theology, as well.

From Encyclopedia to Narrative

Several years ago, when I read *A New Kind of Christian* by Brian McLaren, my faith was shaken. I finished the book with far more questions than I had when I began reading. One of my struggles was how to regard the Bible. I wondered, "Is it some sort of manual for living or is it more of a narrative, tracking the interaction between God and humankind, expressed in the culture and understanding of the times?"

I was such a diehard Bible guy that it was difficult for me not to use terms like "verbal", "plenary"[1], and "original manuscripts" in describing what I believed. It was actually difficult for me accept what the Bible says about itself and not try to force it into a framework to fit my theology.

"All Scripture is inspired by God and is useful to teach us what is true and to make us realize what is wrong in our lives. It corrects us when we are wrong and teaches us to do what is right. God uses it to prepare and equip his people to do every good work." (2 Timothy 3:16–17 NLT)[2]

One of the awesome things about this passage is its simple practicality. In essence, it says Scripture teaches us how to live. That is a lot different than the conservative emphasis on dissecting and examining the minutiae of the scriptures and becoming a technician in biblical languages.

The other thing that drove me to the narrative persuasion was the tendency Christians have of picking and choosing which passages they want to take literally, which ones they tend to emphasize, and which ones they ignore. Passages about homosexuality; emphasize them. Passages about women covering their heads in church services and sins like gluttony; not so much.

I was taught that I should read the Bible every day and master its content. It was as if exposure to its words was a magic pill that would make me a better Christian. I hardly missed a day of Bible reading for decades, but it didn't work. I have diligently studied several books of the Bible in depth. I have taught many of them verse-by-verse. At some time or other, I have studied all sixty-six books. That didn't work either.

The Bible is not a magic pill, nor is it a text book for academic research. It is the narrative between God and man throughout the ages. Its lessons are ultimately only meaningful if they are lived out and affect our daily lives. I already have a lot of knowledge, now it is time for me to act on it. But, life is stubborn and these things take time. We humans do a lot of failing. So, we need a lot of grace.

From Guilt to Grace

I think of Jesus' response to the woman who was caught having sex with a man she shouldn't have been having sex with. Scooped up from the bedroom and thrown into the middle of a mob of violent, self-righteous men, she cowered, quivering, ready for the first rock to hit her in the side of the head, wondering how long it would take her to die, and overwhelmed with the weight of a life poorly lived.

Enter Jesus, so drunk with grace he didn't make sense to anyone, but he was deadly serious. He focused on the accusers' sins, rather than the sinner's. He dispensed guilt to the accusers and grace to the sinner. His words for the angry mob, "Let he who is without sin cast the first stone." Of the adulterer, he asked, "Where are you accusers? Didn't even one of them condemn you?" "No, Lord," she said. He replied, "Neither do I. Go and sin no more."

Let's leave the land of self-loathing, which dishonors Christ, and explore the frontier of freedom and grace in the way of Jesus. Here is the good thing, the only good thing, about failure and guilt...it can lead us to the one who has done something about it.

Many years ago, I heard a prominent radio preacher say the goal of the Christian life is to sin less. When I was young (and more optimistic) it made sense to me. After all, we are to become more like God, and he is holy, so we should at least be on the road to improvement. Yet, like so many of the things I was told as a Christian and used to believe, it sounded just a little off to me, but I accepted it anyway.

It seems like a punitive and uninspiring goal, that our purpose in life is to clean up our act. It also seems arrogant to think we can make ourselves like God.

I always felt I must be different than the rest of the people in the Christian faith because I wasn't on some sort of upward trajectory in changing my thoughts, habits and actions for the better. For me, it was more of a step forward, followed by a step backward. Sometimes, I might even take two steps one way or the other, but I never felt as though I was instantaneously, supernaturally delivered from a besetting sin. Thinking other people were miraculously delivered left me feeling pretty depressed.

When I was a pastor, people would often give me an unrequested evaluation of their spiritual lives and they were always guilt ridden. Their responses were always a matter of "more" or "less." "I need to read my Bible more. I need to pray more. I need to witness more. I need to stop losing my temper. I need to stop looking lustfully at other women."

The church's message has been, "You need to fix that." "That" being whatever you feel guilty about, and if you don't feel guilty about it, we'll throw a little guilt your way.

If an alien who secretly landed on earth were to examine Christian books and listen to Christian radio, he would conclude we are a self-consumed, neurotic people bent on attempts at self-improvement.

The church's message to men is even worse. It's emasculating. "Be a good husband and father. Be a good church member. Don't look at porn. Join the men's ministry." The church's milquetoast approach to men basically teaches us to be a good boy, rather than to be the man God made us to be.

Obviously, I am not as in tune with the expectations the church puts on women, except I can see that, historically, it has been totally out-of-step with reality. I have heard sermons on why women should not follow the clothing fashions of the day, should not be in the workplace, should not have a significant church leadership role, and should not do anything their husbands didn't come up with first.

It seems like a strong woman or man who wants to be more than a cog in the wheel of the church's programs is perceived as dangerous.

This kind of Christianity is anything but compelling. It is a negative message about trying to rein in sinful and harmful behavior, but it only increases our sense of guilt and does nothing to improve our behavior. It actually makes us want to engage in some more of that sinful and destructive behavior as a means of relief from the pain of our continued failure at self-reformation.

There is this intuitive understanding of grace that causes people who have little to do with the church to think it should be the most accepting place in the world. But, the church is usually much less accepting than society at large because of our tendency to delineate right and wrong and to condemn sinful behavior in others, rather than to promote a message of grace.

It doesn't sound much like Jesus' message of giving up on attempts at self-reformation, accepting the fact that he has sacrificially paved the way for us to enjoy a relationship with God, giving us immense personal meaning as we join him in his kingdom work.

What has been missing from the church's proclamation is grace and a personal sense of meaning. This is a positive message, a here-and-now message, bringing meaning and fulfillment to our lives. If anything has the power to change those deeply set behavioral patterns in our life, it is grace, not guilt.

Grace is a difficult and profound concept for human beings to understand. We prefer an-eye-for-an-eye, logical sort of judgmentalism.

We have each built our own personal "hall of shame." We have visited it so often that we have the floor plan and each exhibit memorized. We can provide detailed commentary on the nuances of each piece.

Grace obliterates our hall of shameful memories. More than that, it doesn't give just the exact opposite of what we deserve. It doesn't just multiply the blessings and joy that replace our guilt. It surprises us beyond that. Grace doesn't keep score. It doesn't understand math. It uses a totally different metric. It speaks another language.

The degree to which we grasp grace will determine how we see other people. Bums could be prophets. People we think are different from us, actually aren't so different. Every person's story is important. Screw-ups deserve another chance.

Our failures don't just remind us of our helpless stupidity; they also remind us of his grace. The Accuser is accused and we are set free.

The grace we are starving for is always there. Even though we go through all kinds of ups and downs, even though sometimes we walk with Jesus and other times we walk (or run) away from him. Even though sometimes we know we need him and other times we seem to be doing fine on our own; his grace, his love, never changes. We can't scare him away.

From a Sales Pitch to a Way of Life

During my years of re-evaluating my faith, I had a difficult time figuring out how to do evangelism. Some of the things I have been taught seemed like they cheapened the message by making evangelism all about information and presentation. It seems like there was very little consideration for the specific person, my relationship with him or her, or the work of the Holy Spirit in his life.

I remember hearing about the nineteenth century evangelist D.L. Moody sharing the Gospel with one person every day. It sounded well-meaning, but mechanical and arbitrary, as if everything God is doing is dependent upon us. I was even taught how to share the Gospel in seconds by using an illustration. It was so quick; you could use it on a grocery checkout clerk. About thirty years ago, I would go out weekly with a group of men on a "soul-winning" mission as we visited the people who had visited our church.

Finally, I realized the need to transition from a "come and hear" approach to a "go and show" one, from presenting or sharing the Good News to being the good news. I had begun to realize God was at work within everyone, not just church folks. Therefore, it was important to care enough about people to get to know them, so we are working together with what God is already doing, rather than doing our own thing. Honestly, the church's credibility is so bad, we absolutely have to support the good news message with good news living and tangible love. I think it was supposed to be that way all along.

Our message is one of redemption, restoration, and relevance. We are redeemed by Christ and must repent of attempts to try to gain his acceptance; instead accepting that he has sacrificially paved the way for us. We are restored to our original position, a special relationship with God at the pinnacle of his creation. We are not just holding on for heaven, we have a relevant, fulfilling role in his kingdom here and now. If we could latch onto this concept, our life would feel much more exciting. We are fortunate to partner with God on a mission of love, wherever we find people who need some tangible evidence they are loved, and I think that is everyone.

That message is a tad bit different from the message I used to hear a few years ago, which was something like "You're a lowdown sinner. Accept Jesus as your Savior and go to heaven. Pray this prayer. In the meantime, hang on, the world stinks."

Sign me up for that!

"The church doesn't exist for itself; it exists to serve the world. It is not ultimately about the church; it's about all the people God wants to bless through the church. When the church losses sight of this, it loses its heart. This is especially true today in the world we live in where so many people are hostile to the church, many for good reason. We reclaim the church as a blessing machine, not only because that is what Jesus intended from the beginning, but also because serving people is the only way their perceptions of the church are ever going to change."[3]

How did Jesus evangelize? He came and lived among us; a really weird thing for the creator to do for his creation. I cannot imagine what it was like for him to deal with the self-imposed limitations of humanity and the misunderstanding, betrayal, abuse, and torture he endured at the hands of his beloved. Honestly, most of the time, I don't even go somewhere I feel a little uncomfortable.

He was a great lover of people. I have lots of room for improvement in drawing people out, hearing their stories and helping them feel loved. He shared life with them by going to their parties, and crying and laughing with them. I can be a little isolated and insulated.

I am learning I have to be good news, not just talk about it. I need to do life with people and not try to convince them to do something, such as attending my church.

From Axioms to Questions

Even during my last few years as pastor, it seemed to me we had the wrong goal for the Christian life. My Charismatic friends seemed to think it was all about powerful manifestations of God. Speaking in tongues, prophecies, and healings were all the rage. For evangelicals, it seemed to be mostly about knowledge, believing the "right" things. Neither focus seemed to result in much positive life change or have much of an impact for good or for God upon the world. Interestingly, both approaches feed the ego by having a power or knowledge that others did not have. I came to the conclusion that neither group had God nearly as well figured out as they thought they did.

For instance, our knowledge of the Bible can turn into an ugly, unkind, and inhumane thing. It was Arun Gandhi, the grandson of Mahatma Gandhi, who said, "People of the book risk putting the book above people."

I would hear propositional sermons, in which the preacher declared, "If you do this, God will do that for you." My personal life never seemed to bear that out, nor did it follow the patterns the preacher so boldly proclaimed. That teaching didn't even hold up when I thought through various people in the Bible and their life circumstances.

We have taken the mystery out of God and if anyone is mysterious, He is. How can we possibly, rationally say that we have God figured out and he always has to act "this way"? I mean, I don't even have my wife figured out. I don't even have me figured out! How could I possibly figure out the Creator?

If our minds and understanding have limits, and they do, there is a pretty good chance we might be wrong about something concerning our understanding of God. Church history is largely a record of how we got it wrong, but Christians were willing to fight and kill for those things because they believed they were right. They engaged in inquisitions, militaristic crusades, torture, and executions over differences in beliefs.

So, did we suddenly get everything right, just like good church-going people have thought at every epoch of church history?

There needs to be room for questions, because anything true can withstand any sort of questioning we can come up with and people have some good and honest questions about God.

The church should be their sanctuary from fear and exclusion. Their questions should be welcomed, but it is exactly at this point when people often leave the church. They can tell their questions are unwelcome, because the church already has its axioms that must be embraced in order to be an accepted member of the club.

From Religion to Life

I wish Peter Faulk were still living and wearing his crumpled Colombo trench coat. I would love to hear him approach some church leaders at a convention and say, "Excuse me, sir. Just one more question. Did Jesus come to start a religion?"

Good question, detective.

Religions have their sets of beliefs they cling to, their condensed version of truth, how they make sense of things. If you believe them, you're in and if you don't, you're out. The religious disparage those who don't hold their beliefs. Historically, and even currently, some religions persecute, torture, or kill those who differ.

Religions have their buildings as a place for the faithful to gather. They are led by their ordained and trained leaders. They have rituals they perform that generally only have meaning to the initiated. Religions have all of these things, and more, which they regard as sanctified, separate from the rest of the world and sacrosanct, above criticism.

These are things all religions have in common, including Christianity. I just don't see Jesus in this!

My problem with the religion of Christianity is that it is set apart from the rest of life. When I say the word Christianity, you immediately think of church buildings, pastors, offerings, sermons, and worship services, all of which are detached from regular life. Did Jesus die for that?

Jesus was a rebel! The church is producing mild-mannered clones.

Jesus went after the religious big shots with guns a-blazing, because they took advantage of people in the name of religion. They heaped guilt and expectations upon the people, while continuing their pitiful, piteous act.

He didn't complain about the government, which was horribly cruel and corrupt. He focused his scathing comments on his own (religious) house.

He went everywhere he wasn't supposed to go and hung out with everyone he wasn't supposed to associate with. He had compassion for those who were pushed to the fringes of society and focused on those who others ignored. He broke barriers.

He never preached an expository sermon in his life. He told stories. People learned the ways of Jesus by traveling with him.

He loved children. He went to parties. I think he probably told jokes, danced, and drank wine.

He spoke of freedom and practiced forgiveness. He set people free!

That's what I want. Sheesh! What a contrast between life with Jesus and the religion of Christianity!

Here is what drives me nuts about our understanding of Christianity. It is separate from life!

Jesus didn't come to begin another religion! He came to restore our relationship with God and show us how to live! The way of Jesus is something woven and integrated into the very fabric of life. It is not a Sunday thing; it is a 24–7 thing! It is not high and mighty, sanctified and sacrosanct. It's down and dirty.

"I don't follow Jesus because I think Christianity is the best religion. I follow Jesus because he leads me into ultimate reality. He teaches me how to live in tune with how reality really is."[4]

Somehow, I don't think our magnificent church structures, auditoriums, state of the art sound and projection systems, slick, packaged programs, impressive speakers and musicians are what Jesus had in mind for his followers. I look at all of that stuff and ask myself, is that what he died for? I believe he has something far more personal and more transformational in mind.

He is with me when I am loving writing this book, as well as when I wonder why the hell I am spending all of these lonely hours on a project when I have no way of knowing what will become of it. He is with me when my wife and I realize we are deeply in love after 39 years of marriage, as well as when we are ticked off with each other. He is with me when I talk with my Calvinist, but wonderfully congenial neighbor, as well as when I am with my other neighbor who has a terminal lung disease. He is the reason I care, because without him I tend to be too damn selfish and focused on my personal to-do list to care much about anyone else. He is with me when I sat crying with my wife at the funeral of each of her parents. He is the reason I want to get things right-with my parents now that they are in their latter years and have lots of needs.

My whole journey has been to find something real, something that works. That journey led me down countless rabbit hole that I didn't even want to look in. It caused me to question almost every spiritual thought and belief I have ever had. It caused me to turn away from anything I thought was less than solid and authentic and find that God was right there in the midst of this crazy search, because he was everywhere.

How does the church shift toward a faith that is stripped down, integrated into all of life, down and dirty, rebellious and real? Well, there is a lot of work to be done.

I believe that honesty and the Holy Spirit are traveling companions. So, honesty is an excellent place to begin. Someone needs to stand up and say, "We don't have it all figured out. We value you and value living in the way of Jesus more than trying to build an organization. If you don't believe like the rest of us and have a lot of questions, that's cool. You're safe here. Fire away with your questions. We are going to simplify our schedule so you have time to live out the Gospel with the people in your own world. Let's learn how to live and love in the way of Jesus. We are going to starve religion and feed life."

Engage

If I were a senior pastor (again) who was no longer content to do the drill of trying to meet expectations, hoping that people will keep loving me; if I was tired of trying to serve up a buffet of quality programs, while attempting to stay abreast of the latest church trends; if I was weary of trying to keep the sheep happy; then I might take an approach something like this.

Cultivate a Culture of Love.

I would try to create a culture of love; because nothing else speaks louder, nothing else communicates better, nothing else covers up a multitude of errors, and nothing else is more like Jesus than loving people. Think of concentric circles of love, loving one another, loving our community, and loving our enemies.

I would nurture a culture of embracing, friendship, and humor. I would try to make sure everyone had a fantastic time when they were together and make sure they knew they could be who they really are and would still be very much loved.

Then I would take it out to the next circle by encouraging people to be awesome neighbors and co-workers by taking time to visit with their natural acquaintances, being attentive in times of need, and doing things together socially. There would be no ulterior motive, other than just being the good news of Jesus and fulfilling the relational needs we all have. I would gradually free up more time on the church calendar to create more opportunities for these relationships to develop.

This would be a good time to start talking to people in the community about their real needs and how the church can help with those needs. I would be sure to take one or two other church members with me. I have seen churches become really excited about this kind of practical community service, as they adopt a public school, clean up an area of the city, or help the homeless.

As people become serious about loving people beyond their Christian circle of friends, I would invite some un-churched people to visit the church services and then ask for their honest reactions in the presence of several other church leaders. That would be a wake-up call and open the door to other changes as the church expands its perspective beyond itself.

The last circle is a little more difficult. I would ask my congregants to think of people they tend not to like and to think of those who might not hold the church in high regard. Then I would ask, "How can you communicate Jesus' love to them?" This is when it gets real. It may be too much for some people and they might object. So, expect some conflict. But, it is also where people start to become Jesus-like in the way they view people outside of their comfort zone. Hopefully, this would be the motivation for some awesome personal and church ministries, resulting in people from the community being surprised by God's grace.

When people start loving like Jesus, then your church is well on to its way to healing and closing the gap the church/Jesus gap!

Cultivate a Culture of Blessing.

A logical next step would be to talk about giving away the things God has blessed the church with. I would begin by being more focused on small groups or house churches, where friends gather simply to discuss how to live in the way of Jesus and do life together. The next step could be training mentors to walk with people who want to follow Jesus more closely. Investing heavily in their training reinforces the concept of giving the ministry to volunteers.

The other thing that I would progressively give away is the building. I would cultivate community ministry opportunities until the facility becomes like a community center where God's love is lived out. Some people probably won't like it because the building will get beat up and they may not be able to connect the dots to understand the validity of that type of practical ministry.

These changes would open the door to other changes, allowing the church to become more relational and less programmed in its approach to ministry.

Cultivate New Values.

I would be the leader in cultivating the values and atmosphere for what the church is to become until others gradually pick up on it.

Here are some of them.

- You can be yourself. You don't have to pretend. You can talk about things that you didn't know you could talk about in church. People can ask any question they want and not be ostracized.
- We are serious about living life in the way of Jesus and not just talking about it. We know it will take us out of

our comfort zone and we will be relating to all kinds of people.

- We want to help you fulfill your dreams of partnering in Christ's kingdom. We are here to serve you. We are not trying to use you to build an organization.
- We don't have it all figured out and we need help from everyone in the church and a lot of prayer and guidance from the Holy Spirit.

Eventually, the church would likely begin to be receptive toward many of the other "shifts" I mentioned in this section.

Be Careful.

Lastly, I would be bold, and yet, careful. I would be bold in pursuing these essential values. But, I would be careful to cultivate receptivity, so that I was not the pastor with awesome ideas that was fired before the church reached its potential.

I would plant seeds, try to be patient, and do some extra cultivating with a promising group of leaders and future leaders.

Several years ago someone explained the dynamics of church change to me something like this.

All of his life, your entrenched church member has been building the church with his time, talent, and money. He probably has been there through the tenure of several pastors. He has seen the glory days and the hard times and he has been faithful through it all. The concepts about how to build a church have changed a lot since he first became involved. What I am trying to explain to him about giving everything away, changing the focus from the insiders to outsiders, and reaching out to people he might find repulsive, is not something he signed up for.

Picture the church that he has been building as a mountain. He has built it with his finances, sweat, and diehard support. It hasn't been easy, but he stayed faithful. What I am describing to him sounds like a totally different mountain. As a visionary leader, my head is so far in the future, I am already living there.

But, the painful message my faithful, crusty, old church member is hearing is that he has been climbing the wrong mountain all of his life. On top of that, some upstart is telling him he needs to be climbing a different mountain, but he likes the old one better and he has a lot of doubts about the new one. All of this is too much for him to process, accept, and support.

As I go on and on, thrillingly painting a picture of my preferred future, he is growing increasingly upset about being told he has been climbing the wrong mountain all of his life and has serious doubts about the new vision that is being laid out.

I would not change my course of direction, but I would become more nuanced as I considered those who are as troubled by the new direction as I am excited about it.

Crusty, old church members are tough. They're stubborn, and nearly impossible to convince. So, use the strongest power in the world on them. Love them! Don't do it just to get your way. Love them in ways that are meaningful to them, even if they never do come around.

Best case scenario: The crusty, old church member needs some more time to adjust. Worst case scenario: He becomes a thorn in your side.

It would be wise to make sure you have critical mass before making radical changes.

Been there. Done that. Have the bloody t-shirt.

Okay, I made dramatic church transition sound very risky. It is very risky! But, some things are right and worth the risk!

Part 4

An Irreligious Life:

Adjusted to the New Normal

You never change things by fighting the existing reality. To change something, build a new model that makes the existing model obsolete.
- Buckminster Fuller

If you have left church as you have known it, you have lost something that probably needs to be mourned. But, you have gained the opportunity to be true to yourself and assume a new level of responsibility for your life, rather than outsourcing it to an institution. Process the past. If necessary, mourn what you left behind. Then seize the opportunity to be fully alive in the moment, as you have a beautiful opportunity to re-construct an essential part of the foundation of your life.

eleven

Getting Over It

The trite saying, "Just get over it!" usually makes you want to punch someone in the stomach with every ounce of strength you can muster. You think, "If it were only so simple," or, "If only I could." Leaving church as you have known it is a lot to "get over." Let's break it down.

Seeing the Big Picture

Cultural institutions are failing us miserably and that is causing a worldwide season of unrest. Corrupt governments that have been in power for decades are being toppled right and left. Protesters claiming to be the 99%, upset by the widening wealth gap, have "occupied" city centers around the world. Citizens are frustrated with the political paralysis in the United States. In 2010, the number of voters identifying themselves as unaffiliated was greater than those who identified with either political party.[1]

Like so many people, I am more than a little frustrated with these hopelessly broken, but desperately needed institutions of our society.

Social services are so fractured, fragmented, and siloed in their own little world that they compete with each other and have created a confusing and difficult to navigate maze of services. They are focused on funding from grants, donors, and the government, and produce programs measured by output instead of outcome. They are still operating with a Great White Hope mentality, rather than treating people with dignity and partnering with them to help them achieve their own personal goals.

Customer service is laughable if you don't need it and often enraging if you do. It is excessively automated by cheap-ass companies that can afford to lose a customer here or there and simply don't care if they do. Their priority is sales, not service. They hide customer service phone numbers, hoping you will turn to the website FAQ or a troubleshooting forum. When you finally do speak to a person, it is usually an off-shored, underpaid, undertrained, un-empowered customer service representative who can only provide very limited services. If the representative cannot take care of your issue, many companies offer no reasonable recourse. I can only assume they don't care.

Higher education is overpriced and lengthy. It is built on an outdated model, requiring you take certain courses for a "well-rounded education" that puts you in debt for the next twenty years, rather than preparing you for a job.

Our federal government is paralyzed because of the entrenched, extreme views of each party, a serious lack of listening and negotiation skills, and the corruption of big money from corporations and interest groups. It seems our elected representatives no longer even consider the best interest of their own constituents.

Churches are mired in sexual scandals, political involvement, and the building and maintaining of their own little kingdoms while people fail to see their relevance and wonder why they don't resemble Jesus. Hence, their membership, financial support, and influence are all rapidly shrinking.

Institutions are failing, but individual values are also changing. Bigger is no longer better. Something more intimate and more trustworthy, something recommended by a network of friends is preferred. Institutions, corporations, organizations, and their leaders are all viewed with suspicion because they have repeatedly proven they do not usually have our best interest in mind.

Polished and slick programs are suspect because they are obviously designed to illicit a particular response and offer little or no room for interaction. Attempts to be cool or seem relevant are seen through rather quickly.

Distrust, suspicion, and cynicism are the prevalent characteristics of the day. We distrust those institutions and leaders who have betrayed us, and are suspicious of those for whom the verdict is still out.

What is happening in the church is just one part of that big picture. Some people think these shifts in cultural values are a once in a 500-year occurrence that takes several years or even decades to shake out. The church could be undergoing its most significant changes since the Protestant Reformation!

This dissonance has caused considerable exodus from the church. Between sixteen to twenty percent of Americans claim no religious affiliation[2], a number that has doubled since 1990.[3]

Americans who describe themselves as 'unaffiliated' or 'none of the above' has been on a steady increase for fifty years and has now reached 16 to 20 percent. If this trend continues, by 2042, "nones" and adherents of other religions will outnumber Christians.[4]

As a result, significant numbers of people have questioned their faith and even more have questioned their church. Many of these people still embrace Jesus and the idea of church, but simply do not want to be a part of an institution they disagree with. Therefore, a growing segment of the population has opted to describe themselves as "spiritual, but not religious."

This journey usually begins by asking questions. The questions usually make us a little uncomfortable as they threaten some of our long held presuppositions. They make church leaders even more uncomfortable because they ultimately threaten their position of authority, their livelihood, and their sense of identity.

If you are questioning institutional Christianity, you are a part of a massive flow of culture and history at a time of upheaval and transition. The exodus is huge, and you are, by no means, alone!

Mourning Your Loss

If you were a part of the church for a long time and have decided to bow out, you will experience a real sense of personal loss! The mission of the church, and that of your particular local church, was probably something you deeply believed in. Now that you can no longer, in good conscience, support it, you probably feel a little homeless. You need something to believe in, but are convinced church as you have known it is not it. Being unsure of what you believe has left you in a "no man's land," dealing with a void in your life.

Of course, you will eventually find your way, and you're probably not the heretic some people think you are, but right now, there is a gaping hole in your soul.

You need to feel your loss deeply and you need to talk about it. Cry out to God about it. You will probably feel your sense of purpose, direction, and identity threatened for a while, but it will pass.

You may feel angry. I did. I felt as though I was sold a bill of goods. It cost me thousands of dollars to get a "good Bible education" that didn't do me one bit of good when I wasn't a pastor anymore. I had over twenty years of valuable experience, but nobody recognized the transferable skills I had honed for all of those years. I had moved my family all over the Midwest to pastor small churches that had a snowball's chance in hell of becoming vital and relevant. I was maligned when I had "wild ideas" about the church serving the community and being somewhat relevant to the culture. I loved the church, but it left me high and dry. I put all of my eggs into one basket, the church basket, only to have them crushed.

It hurt, I mean, really hurt! At times, I cried out audibly to God asking him just what he was doing.

Mourn your loss and express your anger. It's a big deal. You have the right to be disappointed, hurt, and angry.

David Hayward, a.k.a, The Naked Pastor, has an insightful blog post about his process of leaving church. The post is entitled, "Why is it Hard to Leave the Church?"

"I've left the church. Many times. The last time I left was over two years ago. It was painful every time. Here's just a few of the reasons why it was so difficult to leave.

Fear: When I left the church, a profound cloud of fear enveloped me: "What have I done?" No matter how much you rationalize your decision, the years and years of indoctrination collect to shout out jeers and threats for your selfishness, stupidity, sinfulness, and shortsightedness. You have just willingly divorced yourself from God and his people, taken your first step closer to Hell, thrown yourself into the arms of the Devil, and destined yourself to an endless road of Perdition. You have officially branded yourself a Heretic. Lost! Of course this isn't true, but try telling yourself that! Over and over and over again.

Friends: The first time I left the church I imagined I would keep many of the friends I had there. I learned quickly that it never seems to work out. Even the last time I left the church that fantasy was still burning in my mind. Again, it hasn't worked out. You lose friends. Not all, but most of them. Period. You have to learn how to make new ones while you're grieving the loss of your old ones. Not easy.

Inspiration: There is something inspiring about gathering together with others on pretty much the same page, in agreement, learning together and singing together and supporting each other. I love hearing or delivering a good sermon. Honestly! Most often I walked away refreshed and refueled for the next week. Learning how to do that by yourself is not simple.

Music: I was always involved with the music and worship. The last worship band I had rocked! I loved playing and singing with them. We had some great times and even made a CD together that's pretty good. I haven't picked up my guitar since I left, but that's my fault. I don't listen to worship music much anymore either unless it's renaissance church music or Russian Orthodox choirs. There's too much "ick" associated with worship music for me now.

Support: When I and my family went through difficult times, we always had people around us who cared and actually did something about it. We've been given food, money, babysitting, cars, rides, help moving, prayers, company, words, vacations... you name it. The church also made it easy for us to be generous and give. Now we're on our own, and the difference is noticeable. We are learning to be self-sufficient and generous independently.

Destiny: The last denomination I was involved with was the Vineyard. Prophetic words, words of wisdom, dreams and visions are a huge part of that culture. My life had meaning and a sense of purpose. I woke up every morning pretty much knowing what I had to do and where my life was heading. I had a destiny! Even though I now believe most of that was hype, I did enjoy living in that matrix of illusion. Then I took the red pill. Oh my!

Validation: When you are in the church, you get a strong sense that you are on the gospel train. You are doing the right thing being counted among the people of God. You are a member, and that gives you a sense of assurance that you are indeed saved, that God has his eye on you and that you are on the right track. When you get off that train, you have to build your own sense of assurance that you are okay, and that is an arduous but necessary task.

Boredom: I have so much more time on my hands since I left the church. I remember my first Sunday morning not going. I went for a walk around the time when cars where driving by on their way to church. Did I ever feel strange! It was hard not feeling like a delinquent. A sinner. I've gotten used to it to the point now where I relish my Sunday mornings. But, that's not all. When you involve yourself with the church, it can become like a family with its 24/7 demands. Now I have to be self-directed; but I'm learning.

Children: Even though Lisa and I are learning our new way of life, we always worry about our children. They are amazing young adults. But, they have been exposed to all the crap that's been dealt out to us, and their impression of church is not rosy. We never slam the church in front of them, but they aren't stupid. They catch on. We don't want them erroneously believing that this means we are enemies of religion, the church, faith or spirituality. They each have their own brilliant expressions of spirituality, but it's been forged by fire. Sometimes ours.

Inclusion: I fight hard for the church. Some people mistake it for me fighting hard against it. When pressed, I still say I am a Christian and that I love the church. I totally believe in the right of people to gather together volitionally, but in a healthy manner…which is rare. I am also for spiritual independence. It saddens me when people assume that because I've left the church I am no longer in the game. When I was in the church, my voice was criticized as biting the hand that fed me. Now it is criticized as not deserving to critique something I'm not a part of. Can't win. Teamless.

(Please understand that even though most of these are really good reasons to stay in the church, most often they come at a price. Like the rabbits of Watership Down who were well fed by the farmer. But, the deal was the farmer could occasionally harvest some of them for food and fur. In this case, none of the good the church offers is worth it.)

You might be thinking it is far more dangerous in the church than out. That's true for many! Every church is different. Each of our reasons for leaving is different. I'm just sharing what some of the dangers are for me. Yours could be totally different. Probably are! Bottom line: there can be dangers and we need to be aware of them.

Just a friendly warning. Enjoy your new spiritual life as a hermit!"[5]

Jim Henderson is an entrepreneur, consultant, former pastor, and author of *Jim and Casper Go to Church*. He has been away from the church for twelve years. Contrast what Jim has to say in this blog post entitled, "Church and Me" to David Hayward's words in the previous post.

"Several times each week my wife and I talk about how to redesign church. We've come up with numerous ideas. Here are a couple of them, once-a-month-church which literally only meets once a month and doesn't require a full time pastor. Or here's a church that non-believers wish someone would start tomorrow in their neighborhood, it's called Nothing But Kids, adults serve while the kids do church and the non-believing parents learn the bible by teaching the kids.

What makes these conversations ironic is that I stopped attending church twelve years ago making Barbara and I sound like a couple of dry religious drunks.

However, since I'm also a fairly public part time paid-to-be-Christian my religious life is still more active than most. On most days you'll find me counseling, coaching pastors, leaders, non-Christians to follow God, Jesus and even attend church.

Add to that, that several times a year I'm invited to speak at a church service affording me the opportunity to compare and contrast how church may or may not have changed from what I remember twelve years ago. It might also help you to know that for 25 years prior to dropping out I planted two churches preached several times a week, led mission teams overseas and wrote articles and books about worship, evangelism and leadership.

I say all that to say that from my perspective I get all the church I need. I just don't go to church anymore and no, I don't miss it.

The most common question people ask when the topic of my non-church attendance comes up is what I do for community. It used to be "The Lords Table or Teaching" but those have somehow been replaced with deep concern for community, so let me address that.

I pastored for 25 years, meaning 'I get church' – I understand, the soap operas, the hopes, the idealism, the pain, the disappointment and the periodic sense of satisfaction one experiences as a pastor. I also understand the powerful sense of corporate worship people can experience in some churches.

Biblical community is less about a group of people standing together singing songs in a room from 11–12 and more about a deep sense of commitment to Christ, his cause, each other and last but not least – the people Jesus misses most – The Outsiders. When I was attending church this kind of community was episodic at best. Maybe your experience is different.

It may help you to know that I was not born into the Christian church culture. I parachuted in as a young adult. I thought I was joining a movement, a mission but I discovered that people don't go to church to be on a mission. They attend largely to remind themselves that they're Christians. They attend to feel a sense of belonging to something bigger than themselves and to be inspired to keep going. Many go simply because if they stopped going then their wayward husbands or kids would stop attending. And they prefer making that trade

Using this definition of community it turns out that I have as much biblical community as I need both online and in real time. I even participate in a once a month small group of believers trying to figure life out and how to keep things real with Jesus and His mission. I doubt that many Christians would count that as "church."

What about that scary word Christians love to pull out when all other options have failed– accountability. Accountability can't be legislated, demanded or organized. It can only be experienced between two people who trust each other. I have several people in my life who have "walk in rights", my wife being one of them. They have my permission to tell me whatever they think about me (good or bad) anytime they feel like it. And yes some of these people have "challenged" me about my lack of not belonging to an institutionalized church. I take them very seriously, listen carefully and explain my thinking to them. I don't allow everyone this privilege but in order to keep growing I must provide a few people this right even when I choose to not do what they wish I'd do. I think of them the same way I do about the people who edit my books. I will never publish a book that someone else has not edited. It is impossible for us to edit ourselves. We are too easy on ourselves. We are too idealistic. We avoid pain. Nevertheless I don't accept all the changes editors wish I would.

The good news for my church going friends is this – Most people are not like me. They do attend a church. Many of them really, really like it. Others feel that on balance attending church is the lesser of two evils (at least that's the way some of them explain it). I challenge them back by wondering if they don't trust themselves enough to follow their hearts and walk away. They disagree with me and we keep meeting and praying with each other and laughing about how weird all of us humans are.

Here's what I think. I think I've graduated from church. I carry enough Bible in my heart to keep me busy for the rest of my life. I've had enough encounters with God to nourish my soul till I get to Heaven (or purgatory). I've acquired so many friends who are heartfelt followers of Jesus that I'll never have time to get to all of them and finally, I have so many people depending on me to keep my promise to Jesus that I'll always try to put him first that if I started messing up too much they would chase my ass up one street and down the other until I got back with the program.

I'll bet some of you were with me until I used the word 'ass.' Which of course is exactly why I did it."[6]

While David was still struggling to adjust to his decision and was reflective about the process of leaving the church, Jim was spunky, resigned, and content with his leaving. Both men were pastors, but David has been out of institutional church for two years and Jim for twelve years. It has been eleven years since I pastored and probably about three since we discontinued church attendance entirely. De-toxing, de-constructing, re-constructing, healing, and sorting things out, takes time. So, be patient with the process. Be patient with yourself.

Like David, I missed the extended family the church provided. I missed the sense of validation and destiny that caused me to feel I was doing something significant, something I was well-suited for.

145

As you move into this new phase of your life away from the church, you will discover a void. If you were heavily involved in church, you will have a time void. If you were a financial supporter, you will have a contribution void. If many or most of your relationships were through church, you will have a relationship void. As you re-evaluate your beliefs, you will have a belief void. If your sense of purpose was interwoven with your church work, as mine was, you will have an identity void.

The void presents new freedom and new opportunities, but it also brings some new dangers. It is a vortex that quickly tries to suck something into it. Freedom is a dangerous blessing.

Between leaving the church, leaving the pastorate, being unemployed, and turning away from any relationship that smacked of unhealthiness, I suddenly had a lot of alone time. I needed a lot of it just to process my thoughts and keep my emotions in check, but enough is enough.

I grew fascinated with my new freedom to not be stuck in a relationship that wasn't meaningful. I love the people in my life, but I could use a few more relationships right now. It's different after all of those years of being a pastor who was pulled so many directions that I couldn't get around to everybody.

Don't let the disappointing relationships turn you into a hermit. There's a word for people who have too much time alone with just their thoughts, without the forward motion of productivity and the sweet comfort of friends. The word is "crazy."

I have noticed when people get divorced they tend to gravitate toward either depression, indulgence, or another relationship. These are immediate knee-jerk reactions that happen when you haven't allowed yourself time to process your grief and learn how to deal with your new freedom.

When you leave church, you will probably be tempted to react in ways you will later regret. It's easy to overreact and turn against all expressions of faith. It's easy to become depressed and stuck in a victim mentality. It's easy to quickly rebound and join another group when it isn't really what you are looking for. It's easy to jettison all sense of right and wrong and become a hedonist because you feel God let you down.

Put a moratorium on major decisions or changes for a while. Allow yourself time to adjust to your new reality.

Reordering Your Relationships

When I was doing Communitas Collective, I found a lot of people in their thirties and forties were pulling the plug and saying "enough," as they walked away from the institutional church they had known for so long. Often they were blindsided by the sudden change in their relationships. When I was pastor, some friends (certainly, not all) who earlier couldn't say enough glowing things about me, would quickly turn into bitter critics when I did something they didn't like.

With the changes in my life, my relational well nearly ran dry. My pastor "friends" acted as though I had died, and I never heard from any of them again. I wish they would have reached out to me, but I just had to let it go. If things were reversed, I think I would have reached out to them, but honestly, I didn't take the initiative to make contact with them because by then I was in a different world.

Naturally, some of the people in what remained of our small fellowship were unified only by the church; but a couple of families were great friends. My relationship with them gradually changed. Even now, eleven years later, we are still friends, but we don't see each other much. We simply move in different circles. That's just the way life works.

There were people who hurt me, people who had given me grief along the way and those who actually brought the church down, self-righteously, thinking they were on a mission from God (or something). We talked and talked. All that was left to do was to forgive them, forget the wrongs, and go on.

I could make a long list of people who hurt me. It would include the arrogant pastor from my teenage years who seemed to take every opportunity he could find to run me down. It would include my pastor friend who went from self-proclaimed best friend to not returning my phone calls all in one step. It would also include the head of the local Christian charity who dissed me because I was part of a house church and not a "real" church. I could go on and on, but all I can do is forgive them and get on with life.

Leaving church is difficult enough, but when people turn their back on you because you are no longer a member of the club, it is very hard to deal with. We never truly know how strong a relationship is until it is tested. When people disappoint us like that, we need to decide if we are going to address the issue or just let the person quietly slip out of our life. Honestly, it's painful and troubling. You thought these relationships were strong enough to weather a significant change, but often, they are not.

I was surprised to see how many people who used to be a part of a Charismatic or Pentecostal church were having a bumpy ride leaving church. These folks were usually the victims of spiritual/mental/emotional/relational abuse. They usually wound up being at odds with what "God told" someone, frequently a church leader, and it caused all kinds of grief. That is a toxic, unbiblical environment that needs to be left behind, as soon as possible!

It is almost miraculous to leave church without vilifying anyone and without anyone vilifying you. It is an honest test of faith to move through this passage and remain loving. Some relationships will wither. I don't like it, but that's what happens in life. People move on and tend to associate in the circles of their regular activities. Let them go. If people get nasty and say evil things about you, it was not a healthy relationship to begin with and you will be better off without their company. It's hard. It hurts. But, that's just the way it is.

Why does the church thing work so well for all of those people, but just doesn't connect with you anymore? Probably because something drove you to take a more objective look at it. You're not crazy. Neither are the people who faithfully attend every Sunday. You are just at different places. You are not evil or sliding down the proverbial slippery slope because you left. They are not simpletons because they stayed. I know your life would have been simpler if you still felt at home there and stayed in the church, but you have to decide whether you want a simple and easy life or messy and authentic one.

One of the awesome things for me about leaving, and especially about no longer being a pastor, is having so much more control over my relationships. This may sound a little cold, but I am going to say it anyway. I am not lumped together with people I have to be nice to.

Now, if a relationship is unhealthy, I can end it. I am able to choose who I hang out with and I have found some really cool people. Usually, I am drawn to someone on the fringe, someone who speaks up. As my relational bank emptied, I was able to replenish it with whomever I wanted. I had no restrictions. I have added people from a variety of walks of life and I still have room for more relationships.

I have more time than ever for my family, and that has been one of the best things to come out of my leaving church. We spend all the time we can with our children and grandchildren, and it has been a joy!

There are probably some people you need to forgive. Maybe, there are some people you need to talk to work things out. But, you also have a wide open opportunity to meet a bunch of new people who will enrich your life.

twelve

Rebuilding Your Life

It was really easy for me to tell you what I hated about church and Evangelicalism, but I had a much more difficult time expressing exactly what I was looking for. For a long time I felt sort of lost, and I couldn't seem to figure out how to rebuild.

Figuring Out What You Believe

I remember reading, *A New Kind of Christian* by Brian McLaren. I jokingly said it caused "a new kind of confusion" for me. Everything happened at once. I was out of the pastorate, bouncing around various churches, unfulfilled, and wondering why pastors were so closed-minded. I was also reading books by authors who were reshaping the faith in ways that challenged much of what I believed.

I was uncomfortable attending church and uncomfortable when I finally bowed out completely, yet I had to get out because I felt like a hypocrite. I would usually come away from church services and meetings feeling empty, critical, and a little angry. But, I didn't feel too great about sitting out, either. That took a while.

It would be easier if this transitional phase was just about leaving church and did not involve a total re-evaluation of your faith and beliefs, but the two usually go together. It's inconvenient, and adds to the feeling of being spiritually home-less, but, ultimately, it is a good thing because your beliefs will be more authentic in the end.

When you don't review something for a long time, it becomes outdated. If you are basing your faith on something you embraced when you were a child or when you first came to faith, your perspective has changed. When you re-evaluate, some things will stay the same and others will change.

The problem with our beliefs is they are never re-examined and updated. We may have been taught to do so is heresy, but we probably just never got around to it. Maybe, like a child, we simply accepted what we were told and never questioned it. We never pulled back far enough to gain a new perspective. So, this is your time to question, read, discuss and test your beliefs so you can find what is true, what you truly embrace. You don't have to toe the line anymore.

It is easy to figure out what you are against, but it's more difficult to figure out what you are for. A few years ago, I was trying to figure out what I believed. So, I considered points where my beliefs had changed and then paired each point with my new perspective. It was a helpful exercise that became a blog post entitled, "An Integrated Life."

"Trying to nail down a post-institutional theology and practice is a huge task and by attempting it I am opening myself to misunderstanding. What I have typed out here is in no way meant to denigrate anyone who disagrees with me, but rather it is an attempt to describe what so many people, including myself, are experiencing as we find ourselves following Jesus in a post-institutional church mode.

- A pick-and-choose approach in the name of being biblical is unacceptable. When there is a question about biblical teaching, the life and teaching of Jesus is the ultimate authority.

- The bible is not an encyclopedia for proof texting. It is a narrative between God and man to be understood in its historical and cultural context.
- The differences between unsaved and saved and churched and unchurched people have been exaggerated. God is at work in all people and all cultures.
- Jesus did not begin a new religion, institution, or an organization. He began a new way of understanding God and living life.
- Becoming a disciple of Jesus cannot be reduced to a positive response and prayer upon hearing an encapsulated sales pitch. The process is highly personal and unique to each person. It involves giving up on trying to appease God and believing that Jesus is who he said he was. It includes aligning with his kingdom, aspiring to live life as he taught and modeled, and falling short of that goal with great regularity.
- Evangelism is not something to stress over, nor is it trying to manipulate somebody to do something. It is simply living out the life of Jesus (the Gospel) in synch with God's working in another person's life.
- Church is not an institution or an organization. It is people committed to living life in the way of Jesus, drawing strength from one another and finding fulfillment through joining Christ in his kingdom.
- Our theological understanding is incomplete, and likely off base in several ways. So, we make space for people who ask questions, even about those points that we consider to be pillars of our understanding about God.

A post-institutional lover of Jesus...

- does not have to be associated with a local church to follow Christ. He is free to bask in God's grace as much as the most faithful church member.

- is not immersed in church programs and meetings. He is free to live a totally integrated life, with no dichotomy between the spiritual and the secular or church events and the rest of life.
- does not necessarily go to church on Sunday. He is free from church activities to enjoy a Sabbath, spend time with his family, and live out the Gospel among the people in his world.
- does not have to participate in congregational singing to worship his God. He finds a multitude of ways to worship God with his life every day.
- does not rely upon church programs for his spiritual nurturing. He finds various avenues of reflection, community, and service to live out his faith.
- is not necessarily supporting a local church and its mission endeavors with his finances. He is free to use his money to support kingdom activity as he sees fit.
- does not delegate the spiritual training of his children to those running church programs. He is free to assume responsibility for his children, including their spiritual training.
- is not bound to one group of people. He is free to be a part of community, wherever he finds it.
- does not place himself under another human's authority. He assumes responsibility for his own life before God.

Transitioning into a post-institutional way of following Jesus is a very interesting pilgrimage. It is not the path for everyone, but it is a rapidly growing reality for many people."

Your beliefs will probably be in flux for a while, and that can cause some anxiety. Just try to learn to live with it and relax with your God who loves you no matter what. We need to become accustomed to accepting mystery when we are dealing with God and life. We never will have it all figured out and those who act like they do are the most dangerous people of all.

Developing Your Own Practices

A few years ago, I sat at the table in the local state employment center as the workforce development caseworker explained the Worker Investment Act (the stimulus) grants awarded to re-educate laid-off workers. I took note of who was there. It was mostly males and the average age was about fifty, which made me feel right at home. As they told their stories, I was totally surprised to find out most of them were highly-skilled, long-term employees whose jobs were off-shored. Several of them had to train their own replacements. It was not at all what I expected.

Outsourcing sucks! But, we love it and rely on it. Many of us have for years been outsourcing our spiritual nurture, our worship, our community, our mission, our charitable giving, and our children's spiritual training. It's called church. It's funny how some churches have come to resemble big box stores with their nondescript buildings and a menu of spiritual services. It's spiritual Wal-Mart!

Wal-Mart's goal is to have everything you normally would need to purchase at a good price, so you will do one-stop shopping and not even consider other options. The institutional church would like us to think the same, but we do have options. We need to re-think our spiritual practices and ask ourselves, "Who is really responsible for my spiritual expression?"

Once we leave the church, we have to learn how to live with freedom (and responsibility). It's not all figured out for us like it was when we outsourced our spiritual expression to the church. It is a hard thing for those of us who spent a lot of our life in the church. I don't think we need to obsess over these things, but rather discover them as life unfolds. If our faith is genuine, it will find expression, but it is helpful to think about some of the options before us.

Our options are far more open than they have ever been! We get to choose where, when, and how we worship. Will we worship God as we walk along a nature trail in solitude? Will we worship him in a crowded festival, full of people as we are bombarded with a collage of sound, craftsmanship, and a vast spectrum of unique people and their creations? Will we worship him by serving a neighbor in need? Will we worship him as we share a table with people we love? Will we worship him as we hang out with some friends and muse over the wonder of God and life? Will we create something as an act of worship, a poem, a story, or a song? Like I said, we have a lot of options!

Will we read the Bible or another book to further our spiritual development? Will we journal our thoughts or discuss them with a friend or, perhaps, a few friends?

How will we pray so that it is meaningful and not just a rote act? How will we reflect and gauge our spiritual formation?

What relationships do we have in our lives that enable us to experience community and participate in service? Are we too much of a lone ranger? Do we need to develop new relationships?

What makes our life meaningful? What are we doing that makes us feel alive?

What do we excel at? Are we focusing on those things, or just trying to get by in life?

We don't have to give money to the church, but we can. Will we choose to financially support a Christian or charitable organization that aligns with our values and passion?

What will we teach our children now that we are not relying on the church for that? Will we have regular teaching times or do it on the fly, looking for teachable moments?

How can we be a good neighbor? How will we help the disenfranchised? How will we serve?

Once you stop feeling guilty for not going to church, you will begin to appreciate that you finally can have a real Sabbath rest. Don't let other things crowd it out. You have been given a deposit into your time account. Now, you can take up a new interest you may never have had time for before.

If you were regularly supporting your church, you have been given an actual financial deposit. Now, you can decide what ministries, missions, and causes you want to support. Now, you can serve people in a way that excites you. You have the freedom to create new rhythms, new relationships, and new priorities. Treasure it and use it wisely.

I remember when I first backed away from the institution. People thought I was backing away from the church and from God, which tells me their understanding of both was way, way too narrow. When you think about the core concepts of church: community, encouragement, and mission; it is very broad. You don't have to go to a special building to hear a professional communicator, watch a show, and give them money for it to be the real deal. The opportunities for our spiritual expression are endless!

Why do we act like God only cares about the church, i.e., the institution? We need to remove the blinders and see God at work everywhere, because He is. I used to think most people who weren't church-goers were far from God. Now, I think they are nearer than some church-goers. I used to think music, theater, art, movies, and television were more or less godless, and the good stuff was in the church. Now, I know some church art forms suck and some of the keener spiritual insights are in so-called "secular" art and music. These artists can be real and ask better questions.

There are all kinds of opportunities in each of our lives to serve people and show them the love of Jesus. Plus, the door has been opened to pursue new relationships, new causes, and new ministries. When I first left church as we have known it, I was constantly making new discoveries and I was seeing God everywhere.

My friend, blogger, and pastor, Kathy Escobar has some brilliant ideas about new practices that helped her endure a difficult time of transition.

"...I also wanted to take a little time to center on an oft-overlooked topic in the deconstruction conversation–how do we tend to our souls and our spiritual lives when we're in the midst of so much upheaval?

Sure, many of us might be allergic to some old spiritual practices, but are there new ones that we can try that might help us feel less lonely and disconnected to God in the process? In the same vein, and because they are all tied up together, making sure we are tending to the care of our souls in the process is critically important.

Life in the spiritual desert of deconstruction requires water, rest and food, or we will die.

For me, as I made some shifts away from the utter and total absorption in the megachurch I was part of, I found that some of the things that brought me comfort before no longer did. The Bible felt flat. Worship songs made me go a little nutty. Journaling just felt forced. I longed for connection with God in the-old-ways-that-used-to-work. But, it just wasn't working.

Then something shifted a bit and I began to let go of feeling like I had to grind down to find something I just couldn't find. Instead, I tried to let go of the old (and not feel guilty about it) and began to notice God in other places. I tried to do things that I liked to do, that were good for my soul, that helped me feel rest and peace and connection to God, my soul.

Here were some of these soul care and spiritual practices on this bumpy road:

- I watched a lot of movies. For me, almost the best soul care there is.
- I took one entire day off from meeting or talking with people in any way, shape or form, period.
- My family came up with some weekly rhythms of eating & fun that we all began to honor. It's been awesome.
- I hiked.
- I turned off the radio whenever I drove and put my cell phone in the back seat (I need to start this one back up!)
- Late night conversations with dear friends around fires and kitchen tables and coffee shops.
- I tried to practice the daily examen before I went to sleep or when I was driving alone in the car–where I noticed God in some way, shape or form during each day. (The daily examen is a technique of prayerful reflection on the events of the day in order to detect God's presence and discern his direction for us.)
- I spent as much time as I could on the lake, which is my second-to-the-beach-favorite-place.
- I used The Message translation of the Bible & tried not to compare it to the passages I was used to.
- I started blogging, a really interesting spiritual practice that I think is helpful in getting comfortable in our own skin.
- I read the red letters in the gospels.
- In the last year and a half I started walking every-day-come-rain-or-shine for my back, but now it's one of my best spiritual practices ever."[1]

Like Kathy, I found some new routines, disciplines, and ways to blow off steam to help me settle down from the soul trauma of turning away from the institutional church and the pastorate and venturing into the unknown.

The most natural thing for me was to pray. God and I had a lot of things to talk over. Sometimes I yelled. That's okay. He can handle it.

Writing was the other thing that may have saved my life. I didn't have a congregation to preach to, but I still had some "preaching" to do. That's why I began blogging. At first, a lot of it was raw and angry, but then I became a little more pastoral. I became a part of a community of on-line friends. After a while, I developed a love of writing and started writing about other things. It gave me a new avenue of expression and a sense of purpose.

I needed some activities in which I just checked out of life for a while. Bicycling was one of those things. I almost always ride along Lake Michigan because it's beautiful. The whole experience of the physical exertion, the beauty, and conquering a ride of several miles was always renewing.

I began to enjoy stories more than I ever had before. I read more novels and watched more movies. I let them take me far away from my regular world.

Right now, I have hunger for adventure. The opportunities we have had for travel have been refreshing, as I literally left the normal grind far behind. Last spring, Patty and I took a dream trip down south. We lived on a Florida beach for a week and spent a couple of days each in Nashville, Savannah, and the Smokey Mountains. We had no agenda or plans other than where we spent the night.

I am an intense guy. I want to figure things out and then move on to get something done, but sometimes my personality doesn't fit my life circumstances very well. Finding peace with leaving church and finding my way forward was full of fits and starts and it took a long time. Don't try to get through it overnight. Take some time off and just enjoy life now and then.

thirteen

Creating Tomorrow

Jesus was an irreligious radical who loved outcasts and berated religious insiders. The church today doesn't look much like Jesus and it is leaking people like crazy. A lot of folks have bailed. Now they are trying to figure out their new life of spiritual freedom. That's the Reader's Digest version of all the pages of this book so far, but it is not the end of the story. Now, I am wondering, how do we pull this off? How do we follow Jesus in a post institutional way? What will the church look like in the future? When we consider changing structures of society, I can think of three options.

Rebelling

When I began to disagree with what I was taught, feeling it misrepresented Christ, I was mad. I had been sold a bill of goods. The "bill of goods" cost me thousands of dollars for an education that is now useless. It caused me to move my family all around the Midwest. I became a bit neurotic, trying to keep all of my congregants happy and feeling well-served. I paid for my calling with heartaches, disappointment, and the utter collapse of my dream. So, when I began to identify things that were out of whack with the church; I was pissed!

I complained, ranted, and exposed the sins of the church. My early blogging was painfully raw (that's why I have deleted it.)

Here is the thing about complaining. Everyone gets tired of it. Eventually, I even became tired of my own complaining. It is important to see things as objectively as possible and if what you see is negative, complaining is just a normal thing to do. It is the place to begin, but not the place to end.

Rebellion is an option, but rebellion is about the past and the present; it doesn't take us into the future. Historically, rebellions are usually bloody and often don't give way to something much better than what they overthrew.

There have been plenty of church fights. I don't think it's time to start another one. Continuous rebellion or complaining against the institutional church is not going to improve anything. There has to be another way.

Reforming

A few years ago I worked for a high tech company that designed telephony systems that determined how phone calls are routed. You know, those Interactive Voice Response Systems (IVR's) that drive you nuts when you call your cable company with a problem. I was the account executive for a company that was my employer's first large client and still accounted for about twenty-five percent of their income. The client company obtained contracts with multinational companies and tried to discern the IVR system best suited to their needs. Then our engineers wrote the code to make it happen. We tested the IVR's and they were hosted on our servers.

This was the only client where we did not have direct contact with the company using our systems. The guy I dealt with on a regular basis was a piece of work. He played all kinds of games, lied, and basically did whatever necessary to get the job done. In our company, this business relationship was referred to as a match made in Hell, but it was tolerated and even enabled because there were millions of dollars of business at stake.

It is devilishly hard to change a paradigm when there is money, jobs, and power at stake.

For over twenty years, I was a pastor. Now that I am removed from that scene, I see the church as a bubble in our culture. While some churches are doing great things in their communities, the vast majority of churches' resources are internalized. They emphasize that their members should be worshipped-up, taught-up, fixed-up, and dedicated-up, both in their Christian lives and in support of the church. I find this to be generally ineffective, self-serving, and not much like Jesus.

As I have attempted to venture into social service work and community involvement over the last few years, I found another bubble. Social service agencies are locked into programs that are usually funded by the government or foundations. They measure output, instead of outcome. Their client/provider paradigm is a weird symbiotic relationship in which the client becomes dependent upon the services of the agency and the agency is dependent upon having a steady stream of clients to maintain their funding.

One can wonder what would happen if agencies opted out of the quick fix of the hand-out and treated people like human beings instead of cattle, helping them out with acute needs and working with them to develop and pursue their own plan for improving their lot in life.

I have voted for Republicans and for Democrats. Politicians over promise and under deliver. Seldom do they ever finish well. Political parties are just two more bubbles so locked into ideologies and paradigms that they have paralyzed our government.

My former employer, the church, the social services sector, and political parties are all bubbles within the larger bubble of culture. So, I began thinking about bubbles.

I have never seen an open bubble. It's difficult to get inside of a bubble. People in the bubble have paid their dues. They have drunk the Kool-Aid. They have earned the favor of the other "bubble-ists" by their adherence to the principles of the bubble. Outsiders and newbies may be tolerated, but they will not be heard.

It's hard to see out of a bubble. The rest of the world is seen through a soapy blur of refracted light. Since bubble-ists are secluded in their bubble, they can only speculate about those outside. Some think those outside of the bubble are evil and to be feared and avoided. Certainly, they are outsiders who are ignorant of the ways of the bubble. They "just don't get it."`

So, it's hard to get into and hard to see out of a bubble.

Yet, bubbles are fragile. They must be protected or all will be lost. Therefore, there are guardians of the ways of the bubble who seek to detect dangers, like someone who has different ideas or a person who is asking strange questions. If the bubble breaks, it would be horrible. Bubble-ists could lose their job, their power, their pension, and their sense of significance.

Working within the system is often cited as the only way to change it. I certainly tried to. Honestly, I thought I would be successful and I thought people would listen since there was so much common sense in what I was saying. However, I overlooked a few important points.

If your suggestions challenge the prevailing paradigm, you will not receive a fair hearing because it goes against the prevalent way of thinking. From their perspective, you either just don't get it or you are someone who is angry at the church.

If you are outside of the leadership culture, you will not receive a fair hearing because you have not "paid your dues" to be a part of the inner circle. Some people refer to this as relational capital. I have learned you cannot simply step up with good ideas and passion and expect to be taken seriously in most organizations. You will first have to gain the trust of key individuals and that will take considerable time.

If your suggestions in some way challenge the nature of the organization, you will not receive a fair hearing because people will feel their position, their vocation, and their retirement fund are all threatened.

Reformers are always dealing with a long list of limitations.

Some people may be skilled reformers. I am not. It takes the patience of Job and the realization that you will see small incremental changes at best. However, if you are trying to change the church from the inside, if people are listening, and if you find fulfillment in this approach; then, God bless you! Go for it.

Re-creating

Let's take stock of the line of the reasoning I have suggested, so far.

- There is a huge gap between the kind of life Jesus lived and what the church has become.
- There are plenty of steps existing churches can take to become more Jesus-like and more effective.
- There is a growing number of people who have given up on the institutional church and are simply trying to "be the church" is their daily lives.

  So, what is the next step?

It's easy to see what's wrong with the church. It is even easy to do, as I have done, and make suggestions for improvement. What is hard is doing it.

It takes some serious thinking and personal experience, but it is not that hard to write a personal manifesto about how to be the church without the baggage of the institution. Again, the hard part is doing it.

There is more to be done than tweaking services and programs by making them cooler or more ancient-like. There is something more than starting up a handful of churches for artsy, young adults. There is something other than Internet friendships, though they can be authentic and meaningful. There is something other than beginning house churches which eventually resemble the churches left behind. Somehow, I believe there may be something more than doing church "on the fly" however and whenever; though, that is also valid. I just don't know what that something more is. It feels to me like we are in between things and the next thing has yet to be revealed.

The next step is for gutsy lovers of Jesus to break from the herd and wander into the rich pasture lands of freedom. These paths are where we learn how to love God and man, almost like it's a brand new concept. They will find new ways (or maybe ancient ways) for us to experience community and to join in Christ's kingdom as we shine some of his light in the dark corners of our world, our city, and our circle of friends.

The church is beginning a new chapter and there are only a couple of lines on the first page. So much is yet to be written. I hope to be a part of encouraging people to pick up the pen and begin to write that next chapter.

There are already some pretty interesting sentences showing up on that new page. As Christian America comes to an end, we are seeing a new church develop. It's more accepting and has a place for everybody, including people with questions. It is breaking from the continuous "teach me mode" to do something about real needs in the community and around the world.

In my weaker moments, I wonder if my personal manifesto of the integrated life is enough. I have questions like, "Is there enough community in that type of approach?" "Will I really serve my fellow man in the name of Jesus?" "Or is this just something to hide behind, some sort of one man club for a cranky old dude like me?"

I believe those moments of uncertainty happen because what I have written is an unfinished picture, the crudest of architectural drawings of what will be built in the near future.

I am an organized type of guy, a planner, and a plan writer (something I have done several times in different capacities), but this plan is unfinished.

What's it going to take to write the next sentences in the chapter about blending the way of Jesus with our daily lives?

Let's take a look at some of the required traits.

- A lot of risk taking. People will probably call you a heretic. They will accuse you of being angry at the church. Some of your ideas won't work, but some will be spot on.

- An ability to strip things down to their core. The baggage that goes with the church and Christendom has created the negative caricature. Can we be objective enough to discern each piece that misrepresents Jesus, jettison it, and be able to see and express the beauty in the core reality that remains?

- An intense focus and energy. The simple thing to say is, "I don't like church so I will follow Jesus in my own way." and then become so preoccupied with our daily lives so that we hardly ever give it another thought. There are some hard questions we need to ask ourselves as we assume responsibility for our own spiritual expression. This is a far more challenging path than outsourcing all of this to an institution.

- A commitment to being real. That's why I have turned from the institution. The last thing we need is to come up with another act or something separate from the rest of life.

- Lots of imagination. We need to see beyond the limits of the institution and beyond the tweaks we could offer up. I think there will be ideas as real, as intuitive, as simple, and as beautiful as the ideas Steve Jobs brought to technology. We need dreamers who are also practitioners.
- Courage. It will require trying and failing and trying and failing again and again, until, at last, we stumble onto expressions that work.
- Action. We don't have to have things all figured out to do what is right. The doing will lead to discovering our way forward.

It was Michelangelo who came up with the idea of criticizing by creating and it is a beautiful thing. Another way to think about it is, "Don't try to change the system; make it irrelevant."

The awesome thing about this approach is that all of our energy is focused in a positive direction. We are not doing battle. We are not doing repair work. We are creating.

Henry Ford didn't try to breed a better horse or build a niftier wagon. He revolutionized transportation. Steve Jobs didn't try to make a better CD or improve the design of the cell phone or personal computers; he fundamentally changed the music, communications, and computer industries.

The church doesn't need better Sunday morning services, newer buildings, or hipper pastors; it needs to be totally re-imagined. It sounds kind of weird saying that about the church because of its 2,000 years of history, its defense of the status quo, and the way it has tried to demoralize those who would be change agents; but it is true.

Church history is not over! God is still at work among people on the earth and he cares about each new generation. It's time to write the next chapter!

All of this brings us to this one moment in time, called "the present."

The most important thing in this present tense is the life of Jesus flowing through you and me. That sounds more mystical than I would like, but I am referring to simply meshing faith and life, so one is as everyday as the other. These have to be woven together for either one to have any real meaning.

To borrow a line from Jim Palmer[1], Life is my religion.

Here are some of the details about this "new religion."

It has a motto: Love God and love others.

It has some basic beliefs.

- God has redeemed me. I try not to worry about my sin and failure because that diminishes what he has done.
- God has restored me. I remind myself my relationship with him couldn't possibly be better because it would be impossible to be loved more than I am right now and his love never changes no matter what I do.
- God has "re-purposed" me. I have a vital role to play in what he is doing now, which is an outgrowth of all I am and all I have been through.
- God is at work everywhere and with everyone. I try to notice it, enjoy it, and explore it.
- God has given me an example of how to live. I try to follow the ways of Jesus, though those are some really big shoes to fill.
- God wants me to live out a life of love. I try, but have a long, long way to go.
- God wants me to have companionship and purpose. I try to enjoy it and participate in it wherever I find it.
- God is compassionate to those on the fringes of society. I try to do the same.

Here are some things that are not a part of the "religion."

- There are no organizations, special buildings, paid professionals, sacred rituals, financial overhead, or secret handshakes, because it is a part of life.

- There is no doctrinal statement or systematic theology, because it is integrated into life, not an intellectual exercise.
- There might or might not be regular gatherings because community is important, but it can't be regulated or mandated.
- There is no effort to pull away from culture, but to merge to with it, because God is at work in culture.
- There are no entrance requirements, because we accept everyone and welcome questions.
- There is no outsourcing of my spiritual expression to an institution, because we believe that is an individual's responsibility.

I know is sounds pretty smug to come with my own religion, like it is the only one with without flaw. Actually, I don't think it is new, but it is flawed because I am a part of it. I don't believe I have originated this "religion," nor do I believe I am its only adherent.

I don't like religion. It easily becomes a brand, a club, a belief system, a center of power, a breeding ground for extremists and terrorists who misinterpret it, a way of determining who is in and who is out, and who is right and who is wrong. Religion easily leads to arrogance and hatred.

This is simply my attempt to figure out what I believe. Some of my beliefs are still pretty much conservative Christian ones, just expressed a little differently. Others are kind of radical. After several years of deconstruction, I am re-constructing my faith. What I believe has changed and will continue to do so, but these days I am putting more emphasis on relationships and living out my beliefs.

I confess, these beliefs are somewhat aspirational, but at least I have a sense of direction.

Now is our time to live out a life in which faith and life are indistinguishable from each other. Together they are an incredible mixture.

I tend to be an analytical, process-oriented person who sees the value of plans and systems, but I am increasingly reverting back to the "impatience" of my youth. I don't really think it is impatience, instead, I believe I have mistakenly listened to the voices of the ultra-cautious naysayers (including my own) far too long. So, I have put together a list to help me get started and keep me going. Maybe it will be helpful for you, as well.

- Don't wait for a good opportunity to help a neighbor, just help out whenever there is a need.
- Don't be so concerned about being proper that you miss an opportunity to be loving.
- Don't wait for permission to do something that is right and necessary, just go ahead and do it.
- Don't wait to find a convenient time to do what is in your heart, go ahead, get started.
- Don't wait to get an organization started. You don't need an organization. Do what the organization would do without all of the accompanying hassles.
- Don't wait until it is convenient to do something important because you will always put it off. Do it now.
- Don't overanalyze your idea and be careful how you consider the opinions of others. Some people will think it is their job to find something wrong with it and you will probably be detained or misguided.
- Don't think you have to be so responsible that you must keep suppressing your dream. Get started now.
- Don't get lost in the minutia of life and forget what makes you feel alive. Get started now. The world needs people who feel alive.

- Don't believe people who try to deter you. That's not a loving thing to do. They are probably small thinkers or fear the power within you. Get going.
- Don't even believe yourself when you try to talk yourself out of pursuing that for which you are uniquely suited. You will doubt yourself and your own sanity from time to time. It's normal, but keep going for it.
- Don't give up if you are committed to something. It will be a long and winding road with lot of unforeseen twists and turns. Keep going anyway.
- Don't expect to be praised. You will probably be criticized, if you have a new approach that threatens the old way. Stay at it.
- Don't get overly intense. Your life and your dream will lose their meaning unless you nurture relationships and have some fun along the way.
- Don't spend too much time pointing out what is wrong. Get started on the solution.
- Don't spend too much time criticizing the system; make it irrelevant.

Engage

For Questioners

For those of you who are still in the institutional church, but have some issues with it, if you are being heard and if you are not leaving church mad and frustrated with some regularity; you should probably stay where you are. Just don't ever stop asking good questions. Don't ever stop searching.

For Leavers

For those of you have left the institutional church, you're not crazy or a heretic. You just had occasion to examine things more objectively and didn't like what you found.

Find some other "leavers" because you need each other. You can definitely find them on the Internet, but it would be great to find some in your locality. They may have gone underground, but they are there.

Allow yourself time to process all that has happened to you. It really is a big deal. You have probably lost a lot, like a sense of purpose and identity, friends, and some long-held beliefs. Do whatever you need to do to process it; talk about it, express your anger, and resolve any loose ends and relational issues.

Enjoy your new freedom to rediscover what it means to follow Christ and to join with him in his kingdom. Take a chill pill and dive into life. Make new discoveries about how God is at work in the world. Develop a sense of humor; God has one.

Fill your new vacuum with new friends, new experiences, and new causes as you assume responsibility for your own spiritual expression.

Remember freedom is a dangerous blessing. You could spend the rest of your life being bitter. You could turn your back on Jesus as well as the church. You could become a lazy, nominal Jesus follower. Or you could enjoy a life of love, grace, freedom, and fulfillment by living from your heart and fulfilling your niche in his kingdom.

For Former Pastors

For those of you who used to be on a church staff, if you really were a pastor, you still are a pastor. If you really were a leader, you still are a leader. The way you pastor and the way you lead will change and who you pastor and who you lead will change. Just be true to yourself and don't think all is lost.

Like everyone else who is freed from the institution, you have new freedom to be yourself. Actually, you have even more new freedom than most because you don't have all of those crazy expectations to live up to anymore.

My heart goes out to you if you don't have a back-up plan for employment. You might need to go back to school, but you have the opportunity to do something meaningful without all of the baggage that comes with serving a church. It might be some aspect of your pastoral service that directs you to your new future. Maybe you loved counseling, writing, pastoral care, management, or community involvement. Build a new life that is even more Kingdom-centered and true to who you were created to be.

For Current Pastors and Church Leaders

Congratulations, if you made it through the book without throwing it against the wall! Please, please open your heart to those who feel shut out by your church. If you nurture a truly loving community that welcomes in new people and if you help people fulfill their God-given potential, your church is well on its way. Think about building people, not an organization. Bless the people in your community by giving away everything you can as you live out Jesus' love.

For "Nones"

For those of you who are not involved in a church and maybe, never have been; don't confuse Jesus and the church. I know Jesus needs a better PR team, but not everything that has come out of the church is a disaster. It's a mish-mash because it is a human institutional expression that has had two thousand years to develop its organizational, subcultural, and hierarchical baggage.

If you haven't looked into Jesus, check him out. But, be prepared, he's a revolutionary who loves people on the fringes and lets it rip on the self-righteous. He will challenge you far more than any doctrine that has ever come out of the church.

For Everybody

I leave you with these inspiring words from Justin Zoradi of *These Numbers Have Faces,* to help launch you into your new life of doing what is really in your heart.

"A friend told me that while he hated bussing tables at the restaurant where he was working, he was still waiting for God to tell him what to do with his life. He believed that if he was patient enough and did his work well, eventually God would reveal his true calling.

I told him I don't think God works like that.

We all want to do meaningful work and find our passion, but I can guarantee you this: Your purpose in life will never be written on the wall. And it will never be revealed to you in full.

I watched a brilliant video recently where some Danish filmmakers did a bunch of really stupid things and slowed them down to 2,500 frames a second. They blew up microwaves, chain-sawed coke bottles, and at the very end, pricked a tiny hole in a waterbed. At first, nothing really happened. A few drops of water spilled out. But in a matter of seconds, 200 gallons exploded from that tiny hole, flooding the bedroom.

You want to do meaningful work? Stop sitting on your hands waiting for God to tell you what to do.

No matter how lofty, unattainable, or idealistic, choose that one thing that keeps you up at night and stick a pin through it. Only then can the tidal wave of God's glory and purpose flood your bedroom.

It seems like a lot of people are walking around holding that pin, scared to commit to putting it somewhere. Many people die holding it, their purpose and passion endlessly prayed for but never pursued.

I believe God joins us only when we take that initial risk. If you have a tiny twinge of passion toward anything, you have to jump right through it on your own. It is there that God will meet you."[2]

Contact Glenn

If I can be of help to you, your church, or group,
just let me know.

glennhager.com
glennhager1@gmail.com
847.757.7077

Notes

Chapter 1: Impatient Novice

1. Calvinism can be briefly summarized as believing in predestination, the total depravity of man, and the sovereignty of God.
2. Dispensationalism is the belief God has a different framework for different times in human history, including the imminent rapture of believers from the earth, a coming Great Tribulation, and the eventual earthly millennial reign of Christ.

Chapter 2: Dyed-in-the-wool Insider

1. George Barna is the founder of the Barna Research Group (now The Barna Group) and helped it become the nation's leading marketing research firm focused on the intersection of faith and culture. He has written 48 books, mostly addressing leadership, trends, church health and spiritual development.

Chapter 4: Confirmed Outsider

1. Narrative Theology is a late 20th century theological development which supported the idea that the Church's use of the Bible should focus on a narrative presentation of the faith, rather than on the development of a systematic theology.

2. Communitas Collective was an internet community of people who questioned or left the institutional church. People from around the world contributed articles on a rotating basis. It became a podcast hosted by Erik Guzman and myself and was on the Internet from 2008-2012.

Chapter 5: Authority Problem?
1. Matthew 22:15-22.
2. Matthew 23:13-27.
3. Mark 3:1-6.
4. Mark 2:23-28.
5. Luke 15:1-2.

Chapter 6: Loser Lover
1. Michael Spencer, *Churchianity* (Colorado Springs, CO: Waterbrook, 2010), 52.
2. Philip Yancey, *The Jesus I Never Knew* (Grand Rapids, MI: Zondervan, 1995), 89.
3. Ibid.
4. Michael Spencer, *Churchianity* (Colorado Springs, CO: Waterbrook, 2010), 84.

Part 3 - An Irreligious Church: Shifted into Reality (Introduction)
1. Randy McRoberts, "Demise and Rebirth," *Bible Study Geek*, accessed September 12, 2012, http://biblestudy-geek.com/?s=demise+and+rebirth.

Chapter 8: A New Framework
1. David Kinnaman & Gabe Lyons, *Unchristian* (Grand Rapids, MI: Baker Books, 2007), 29.
2. Gabe Lyons, *The Next Christians* (New York, NY: Doubleday, 2010), 22-23.

3. George Barna, *Revolution* (Wheaton, IL: BarnaBooks, 2005), 49.

Chapter 9: Right Side Up
1. I Corinthians 8:1
2. Frank Viola & George Barna, *Pagan Christianity* (Carol Stream, IL: BarnaBooks, 2008), 14.
3. Ibid, 41.

Chapter 10: Stop Believing, Start Living
1. Plenary means that all parts of the Bible are equally authoritative. This includes such things as the genealogies of the Old Testament. All parts of the Bible are of divine origin.
2. Holy Bible, New Living Translation (Wheaton, IL: Tyndale House Publishers, Inc., 1996).
3. Rob Bell, Velvet Elvis (Grand Rapids, MI: Zondervan, 2005) 165-166.
4. Ibid, 83.
5. George Barna, Revolution (Wheaton, IL: BarnaBooks, 2005), 26.

Chapter 11: Getting Over It
1. Diane Butler Bass, *Christianity After Religion: The End of the Church and the Birth of New Spiritual Awakening* (New York, NY: HarperCollins, 2012), 84.
2. Ibid, 46.
3. Jon Meacham, "The End of Christina America", *Newsweek,* April 3, 2009, 1.
4. Diane Butler Bass, *Christianity After Religion: The End of the Church and the Birth of New Spiritual Awakening,* (New York, NY: HarperCollins, 2012), 46.

5. David Hayward, "Why it is Hard to Leave the Church", *Nakedpastor* (blog), September 10, 2012 (2:10 PM), http://www.nakedpastor.com/2012/07/22/why-it-is-hard-to-leave-the-church, July 22, 2012.
6. Jim Henderson, "Church and Me," *Jim Henderson Presents* (blog), September 10, 2012 (3:30 PM), http://jimhendersonpresents.com/church-and-me, August 7, 2012.

Chapter 12: Rebuilding Our Life
1. Kathy Escobar, "Soul Care and Spiritual Practices for Deconstruction," *Kathy Escobar: Pastor, Writer, Advocate, Mommy, Rule-breaker, Dreamer* (blog), September 12, 2012 (2:15 PM), http://kathyescobar.com/2012/05/02/soul-care-spiritual-practices-for-deconstruction, May 2, 2012

Chapter 13: Creating Tomorrow
1. Jim Palmer is the author of *Divine Nobodies, Wide Open Spaces, and Being Jesus in Nashville.*
2. Justin Zoradi, "Stop Waiting for God to Tell You What to do with Your Life," *JasonZoradi.com: You Were Made for These Times* (blog), September 12, 2012 (4:10 PM), http://justinzoradi.com/stop-waiting-for-god, August 2, 2012.

Made in the USA
Charleston, SC
01 April 2014